THE DEBT
SURVIVAL KIT

THE DEBT SURVIVAL KIT

How to Settle Your Debts Yourself and Save Money

CHRISTOPHER SCULLY

ISBN 978-0-615-31964-3

Contents

Disclaimer

I am not an attorney. I am not an accountant or tax expert. I am not a financial planner or any kind of stock, bond, or mutual fund expert. I leave all of these things to professionals in those fields. What I am is an expert in the field of debt settlement. I have been directly involved with all aspects of consumer debt settlement for over ten years. I have helped hundreds of families through this process, and this kit is intended to be an accurate description of the subject of debt settlement as of the time of its writing.

This kit is not intended as legal advice, tax advice, or investment advice. Creditors change the way they do business whenever they please. New rules and regulations are handed down by state and federal governments all the time. These changes can affect the accuracy and/or workability of the information presented here. Therefore, this kit is presented with no warranty of any kind.

Introduction

Consumer debt, particularly credit card debt, is at an all time high in the United States. Most Americans view credit cards as a way to get by when things are tight. However, if you lose income due to unemployment, accident, illness, divorce, or some other reason, you will soon find yourself between the proverbial rock and hard place. If you can't keep up with your debt payments, you need help. If you don't do something to get the situation under control, the financial mess will get bigger and bigger. There is a way out of this kind of mess—debt settlement. For some people debt settlement is the only solution, short of bankruptcy. You can sign up with a debt settlement company and pay them to settle your debts, or you can do it yourself. I will show you how.

What is Debt Settlement?

Debt settlement, also called debt negotiation, is a method of debt management in which an agreement is made with a creditor to accept some amount less than the full balance as payment in full on a debt.

Debt settlement is useful for eliminating *unsecured debt*. Unsecured debt is a debt that is not tied to any property. Some debts are tied to real property, such as a house or vacant land. Other debts are tied to personal property, such as a car, a refrigerator, or the like. Debts that are tied to any kind of property are s*ecured debts*. Secured debts are not usually candidates for debt settlement because the creditor will often take the property if you default on the debt. Sometimes secured debts can become unsecured debts or be treated like unsecured debts. The most common situation where this can happen is with a car that is repossessed. Often the loan company will auction the car and then try to collect the difference between the auction price and the loan balance from the borrower. These debts can be settled.

There are numerous companies around the country that provide debt settlement services. Most of these companies charge quite a bit of money for their services. Fees of 15 to 20 percent of the total amount of debt are not unheard of. There are a number of good debt settlement companies out there who are helping people get out of debt. The question is do you need to work with a debt settlement company, or can you do it yourself? The answer is you can do it yourself if you have the determination and the knowledge to do so. This kit will provide you with knowledge. You must provide the determination. Along with the knowledge and the determination, you should also be organized. This will make the whole process much easier. If you are the type of person who dislikes conflict or would simply rather not put in the time and energy necessary to settle your debt yourself, you should seek the help of a debt settlement company. Whether you choose to go ahead and settle your own debt or to hire a settlement company to do it for you, this kit will help you.

Since you have purchased this kit, I am going to assume you've researched the other options for resolving your debt problem and have determined that debt settlement is the appropriate solution for you.

How to Use This Kit

This kit is designed so that each chapter gives you a complete understanding of the subject of that chapter. This means you can skip around if you need to. Let's say, for example, that you're already getting a lot of creditor calls. By all means, go straight to the chapter on dealing with creditors. Everyone should read the entire kit. There is a great deal of very helpful information here. Read it in the order that interests you, and good luck with your debt settlement efforts!

If you have questions that aren't answered in this book, feel free to e-mail me at debtsurvival@thedebtsolution.com.

Chapter 1

Debt Settlement Pros and Cons

If you listen to radio in a major city these days, it's hard to miss the ads from various companies saying they'll get you out of debt, cut your monthly payment by up to 50 percent, or settle your accounts for 50 cents on the dollar. Some of these ads are from debt settlement firms and some are from credit counseling firms. Debt settlement and credit counseling are two different approaches to dealing with debt issues. Neither approach is right for everyone.

Credit counseling is the preferred approach for those who need to lower their monthly payments by a relatively small amount or who want to take advantage of interest rate reductions often available through these programs to get out of debt faster. When you enroll in one of these programs, you send the credit counseling firm a single monthly payment, and it in turn makes monthly payments to your creditors. The minimum monthly payment requirement is based on the minimum monthly amount the creditors will accept on the program. If you cannot make the minimum monthly payment, you will not be able to participate in a credit counseling program.

Debt settlement is for people who are unable to make the minimum monthly payments on their debts and cannot afford the required payment for credit counseling programs. People who experienced a long-term loss of income for any reason are good candidates for debt settlement. Debt settlement, particularly if you do it yourself, is very flexible in terms of how much money you need to come up with on a monthly basis. The more money you have in your budget for settlement, the shorter the time frame for settling all of your debts. If you're really tight on funds, it will take longer. If you work with debt settlement counselors, they may require a minimum amount because they have to consider the cost of servicing their clients and so forth. They have to make a profit. The minimum amount of funds most debt settlement companies require is usually much lower than the minimum required for credit counseling.

Bankruptcy, in my personal opinion, is an option that should be held in reserve in case other methods of resolving your debt problems fail.

Debt Settlement Pros

Debt settlement can be an attractive and very beneficial solution to people who are in debt and have experienced a long-term loss of income. Here are some of advantages debt settlement offers to people in this situation.

1. It is possible to save 40–60 percent or more on your debts through debt settlement. If your total unsecured debt is $15,000, you could end up settling all of it for $6,000 or even less. There are no guarantees. Any debt settlement company that says it can promise a specific savings is engaging in deceptive marketing. In my view, any savings is a benefit. If I owe $15,000 and have to pay $14,000 to settle all of it, I'm still ahead by $1,000.

2. Debt settlement programs offer much more flexibility than do other methods of dealing with a financial hardship. Your program is, for the most part, based on what you can afford. A certain amount of common sense has to be applied here. If you owe $100,000 and can only afford

It is possible to save 40–60 percent or more on your debts through debt settlement.

$50 per month toward that debt, you're probably not going to succeed.

3. With debt settlement, the consumer has greater control over the entire process. If you hire a debt settlement company, its employees will make settlement offers when you have the funds for settlement. The creditors don't dictate when or how to settle. The creditors can say that they will only settle for a certain amount, but the settlement company or the consumer can decide whether or not that amount is acceptable If not, end the negotiations at that point and move on to the next creditor.

Debt Settlement Cons

Debt settlement is not a risk-free activity. In fact, there are several important risks I need to make you aware of.

1. Debt settlement does result in derogatory items being placed on your credit report. All accounts that go more than thirty days past due will be reported as delinquent accounts to the credit bureaus. The longer an account is delinquent, the more late payments will be reflected on the credit report for that account. If an account is sent to a collection agency, this is also usually reported on your credit report and is a negative item. Your accounts may be charged off by your creditors, and these "charge offs" are usually reported to the credit bureaus. When accounts are settled, creditors usually report to the credit bureaus in one of the following ways: "Settlement accepted on this account" or "Settled in full for less than the full balance." These negative statements may stay on your credit report for up to seven years.

2. If the amount of debt forgiven in a settlement is more than $600, your creditors must report it to the IRS on a form 1099C as "Forgiveness of Indebtedness Income." According to information on the IRS website, this income can be excluded from your income tax under certain conditions. I am not a tax expert, so you should consult a tax professional for the details on how this works. If you normally do your own tax returns, I advise you to have a professional tax preparer do your returns while you are getting yourself through a debt settlement program.

3. Your creditors will not stop or hold off on collection actions while you are accumulating funds to eventually settle your debts. You will get collection calls and letters from your original creditors. You will eventually get collection calls and letters from collection agencies and/or collection attorneys.

4. You *can* be sued by your creditors or collection agencies. Some creditors may take you to arbitration if that is part of your contract with the creditor. Depending on the laws of your state, if a creditor succeeds in getting a judgment against you, there are various actions that may be taken to seize your money or property to satisfy the debt. You should consult an attorney in your area for the specifics on what those actions might be. I am not an attorney and this kit is not intended to provide legal advice.

5. Interest and penalties are likely to continue to accrue on your accounts until they are settled. Though it is important that you are aware of this fact before you consider embarking on a program to settle your own debt, you must also realize that when it comes time to settle the account, you can negotiate these additional charges away.

6. I have from time to time been asked if it's a good idea to keep one credit card in good standing for "emergencies." This is not advisable. The reason for this is that creditors and collectors may review your credit report when considering a settlement offer. I have seen creditors flat out refuse to settle if there was an active credit card account that was in good standing.

   The best way to approach "emergencies" is to plan for them in your monthly budget. Home repairs, car repairs, and medical expenses can be planned for and you can put money away for these things every month. You should put money aside for those things every month and only use those funds for their intended purpose. I cover this subject in detail in Chapter 5.

Should You Do It Yourself?

You can settle your debt yourself. Whether you should do so or not depends on what is most important to you. Settling your own debt using the methods I give in this book takes an investment of your time.

It requires you to put in some effort into organizing your finances (and records). It also requires a bit of a thick skin.

Debt settlement companies do a lot of the work for you. This allows you to focus on making money and living your life. They take care of the details for you. They, of course, charge fees for their services.

I sometimes use an analogy to help people determine whether to use a debt settlement company or to do it themselves. Consider debt settlement similar to painting an entire house, inside and outside. Even if you have never painted a house before, you could to it all yourself or as a family project. It can be fun and rewarding to do so. Doing it yourself also saves you cash. Your expenses are limited to the cost of the paint, paint brushes, rollers, tarps, etc. that you will need to get the job done. If you don't know anything about painting and want to do a good job, you need to spend some time finding out how to do it right. There are lots of do-it-yourself guides available in bookstores or online. Your local home improvement store may have free seminars you can attend. Once you know what to do, you have to put in the time to do the work. If you have a full-time job that means you'll be doing it part-time on the weekends. If you stick to it, you will get your house painted exactly the way you want. You will also have the pride that you did it yourself and saved money. There are also professional painters you can pay who will paint the house the exact colors you want and all you have to do is pay their fees (including the cost of paint and materials) and more or less stay out of their way. They will get the job done in a relatively short period of time because they will do it full time and they are experienced at painting. As in any business, there are good painters and poor painters so you want to do a little checking before you decide to hire a particular one.

If you would rather paint a house yourself rather than hire a painter, you might prefer to settle your own debt. If you're more inclined to hire a painter, you might be better off hiring a debt settlement company to settle your debts.

Here are a few other questions to help you determine whether or not you should settle your own debt:

1. Can you make time during the day to contact creditors and negotiate settlements during regular business hours?

2. Do you prefer to keep your financial records neat, tidy, and filed?

3. Do you enjoy learning new things and developing new skills?

4. Are you a good communicator?

5. Is saving money more important to you than saving time and/or effort?

If you answered yes to the majority of the above questions, you will very likely be successful in settling your own debt. If you answered no to the majority of these questions, you will have a much more difficult time settling your own debt and are probably better off hiring a debt settlement company to do it for you.

Chapter 2

Creditors and the Collection Process

In this chapter I'll explain how the collection process works. First, I'll identify the players and clarify the terms I will be using when referring to them. The terms and their meanings are often confused, so I want to clarify how I will be using them from this point forward. Definitions of other terms used in debt collection and debt settlement can be found in the glossary.

The Players and Terms

When someone lends you money, he or she is your *creditor* and you become a *debtor*. A creditor is any person or company that grants credit and/or lends money. This includes home loans, car loans, personal loans, and credit cards. Throughout the rest of this kit, the term *creditor* will refer to the company that originally gave you the credit.

It's very important to understand that when you have a credit account with a bank or other lender, that account is considered an asset for that creditor. An asset is something that has value. In the case of your credit card, for example, the value is the balance you owe and, more importantly, the interest they will collect on that balance. When you make your payments according to the terms of the loan or credit card, the bank is making money and the account is considered a *performing asset*. That's a very good thing for the bank. When you don't pay, the asset becomes a *non-performing asset*. That's a bad thing for the bank. If they have too many of those, the government could step in and take actions to remedy the situation, possibly even take over the bank.

A *collector* is anyone engaged in the activity of debt collection on behalf of another person or company. They are not the *creditor*. Collectors are often referred to as collection agencies as well. While this definition is fairly clear on its own, there are categories of collectors that must be understood. One category of collector is the type that collects debt on a commission basis. These collectors keep a percentage of what they collect and send the rest to the creditor. The other category of collector is the type that purchases delinquent accounts from creditors and proceeds to collect on those debts. Anything they make over and above the price they paid for the account and their collection costs is their profit. From a settlement point of view, the collector that purchased the debt is more likely to negotiate and settle an account as long as they can make a profit. They buy debts in bulk at discounted rates. They may pay anywhere from 7 cents to 30 cents on the dollar. Therefore they are often willing to settle for 20 to 50 percent of the balance of the account. Sometimes these debt buyers hire commission-type agencies to collect for them, rather than trying to collect on the debts themselves. Agencies collecting for commissions on behalf of the debt owner are usually given guidelines restricting settlement percentages and terms the debt owner is willing to accept. Some agencies will submit settlement proposals to their clients for approval on settlement terms that are outside the guidelines. You will learn about how to get them to do that later in this kit.

Unfortunately there really isn't any way to tell from a letter or phone call whether or not the collection agency contacting you is a debt buyer. I'll tell you how to get this information from a collector in Chapter 7. That's when it's important to be able to distinguish between the two. There is a clue you may get in a phone message or letter. If collectors say they are contacting you on "behalf of" a creditor, it frequently indicates that the creditor still owns the debt. If they say they're contacting you concerning your _____ account, it could be either type of collector. Throughout the rest of the kit, I will use the following terminology in referring to debt collectors:

- *Collector* will be used when the information given applies to all debt collectors, whether or not they have purchased the debt.

- *Collection agency* will be used to refer to those collectors who are collecting on behalf of the debt owner (either the original creditor or a debt buyer) for a commission.

- *Debt buyer* will be used to refer to those collectors who purchase debt and make their profits based on the difference between what they collect and what they spend to buy it.

The Collection Process

There is a set of activities that are set into motion when a debt becomes delinquent. Most creditors define delinquent as thirty days or more past due. This section will describe the various activities that occur at different stages of delinquency. They are all part of the collection process. Most creditors follow the same patterns with slight variations on their internal policies. Creditors usually don't pay much attention to accounts that are less than thirty days late.

Once an account is more than thirty days late, it goes to the bank's internal collection department. The staff will send you a letter telling you that if you don't pay, your credit will be damaged and you might get a phone call. Collection efforts from the creditor at this stage are not particularly heavy because bank statistics show that 50 percent of these accounts are brought current by the debtor without action from the bank. As your account gets further and further behind, the creditor's collection department will become more active in trying to get you to pay the delinquent amount and bring the account current. This is an important point. They are not trying to get you to pay the account in full. They are trying to get you to bring it current at this stage. If you start getting calls from a creditor, you will usually be speaking to someone who has very little training or experience whose only job is to get your account current. This person has NO authority to settle. Collection department employees often get paid commissions on the money they bring in, which is a major motivation to just try to get you to pay right away. Many creditors divide up their collection staff by level of delinquency. They might have

If you start getting calls from a creditor, you will usually be speaking to someone who has very little training or experience whose only job is to get your account current. This person has NO authority to settle.

a group that deals with accounts that are less than 60 days past due, another that works on the 60- to 90-day accounts, and yet another that works the 90- to 120-days-past-due accounts. There are a few creditors that will start considering settlements around 90 days past due. Most won't consider settlements until the account is much further behind. This is a point of policy set by the individual creditor. After an account is more than six months past due, the banks are required to charge off the account. The charge off is very important to banks. Government regulators look at the ratio of total assets compared to assets that are not performing and/or have been charged off. Most creditors would rather settle a debt than charge it off. You usually get the best settlements from creditors right before they have to charge off the account.

If you don't settle with the creditor before he or she has to charge off your account, the amount of your debt is removed from the creditor's asset totals and is considered a loss. Anything that creditors collect after the account is charged off reduces the amount of the loss on their books.

In my experience there are four general courses of action creditors take after they charge off an account:

- The creditor may send the account to an internal unit or a subsidiary to continue collection efforts in order to recover the loss. Some creditors have recovery units that will continue trying to collect on charged off accounts for years after charge-off.

- The creditor may hire a collection agency to collect on the account for a commission.

- The creditor may refer the account to the company's internal legal department if it has one or to a contracted law firm to pursue legal action against the debtor. In some cases they will follow through with a lawsuit, and in some cases they will not. There is really no way to accurately predict what will occur when an account is sent to an attorney. Many creditors use a mathematical formula or specialized computer program to determine whether or not they will actually carry through with a lawsuit. No matter how they make the determination, they evaluate whether or not they think they are likely to be able to collect enough money from you to make it worth the effort and expense of suing. If not, they won't do it.

- They may sell the account to a debt buyer. This decision is also usually based on a pre-determined formula or computer program. Creditors incur expenses when they try to collect on charged-off accounts using any of the above approaches. If they feel their bottom line would be better if they just sold the account than it would be if they tried to collect on it, they will sell it pretty quickly.

Creditors may try one of the above approaches, then another, and so on. Some may run through all of them and sell the account only after they have attempted to collect using the other three approaches and failed. Creditors can and do sell accounts after they have sued a debtor and won a judgment against that debtor. These kinds of accounts can be sold for more money than an account that's just XYZ days past due and has been charged off.

Once an account is charged off it may jump from collector to collector to collector. It may be bought and sold several times before you are able to settle it. This movement can sometimes make it difficult to reach the person who has authority to negotiate a settlement on your account. I have seen accounts pass through over a half-dozen collectors between the time they charged off and the time funds were available to settle them.

Settlements can be reached with a creditor, collection agency, or debt buyer at any stage in the collection process. Some of the details of the negotiations may be different depending on what the creditor has done with the charged-off account as above. All unsecured debts can potentially be settled if you work at it a bit.

Chapter 3

The Fair Debt Collection Practices Act

IMPORTANT: As stated at the beginning of this kit, I am not an attorney and this kit is not intended to give legal advice. The information in this chapter is a summary of the federal regulation based on my understanding of the law. If you have any further questions, refer to the full text of the law in Appendix A or consult an attorney.

There is a federal law that regulates the actions of collectors. It's called the Fair Debt Collection Practices Act (FDCPA). The Fair Debt Collection Practices Act is enforced by the Federal Trade Commission. This chapter informs you of the main provisions of this law so you can use it when dealing with creditors. The full text of the law can be found in Appendix A.

Many collectors knowingly violate this law. They know that most consumers are ignorant of this law and therefore will not report their violations to the authorities.

Some states may have laws at the state level that afford consumers even greater protections than are provided by the FDCPA. State laws are generally enforced by the state's attorney general.

This law applies to anyone who regularly collects debts owed to others, including collection agencies, lawyers who collect debts, and companies that buy debts. The creditor that issued the credit to you is not subject to this regulation because they are collecting on the debt that is owed to them, not to someone else.

Also, this law applies to personal debts such as credit cards, medical bills, car loans, and mortgages. It does not apply to business debts.

Contacting the Debtor

The law allows a collector to make reasonable efforts to communicate with a debtor about a debt. However, there are some restrictions about what is considered reasonable. Collectors may not contact you at inconvenient times or places, such as before 8 AM or after 9 PM, unless you agree to such contact. If collectors are told orally or in writing that you are not allowed to receive such calls at work, they may not thereafter contact you at work. Additionally, if you are represented by an attorney and that fact is made known to collectors, they must contact your attorney instead of contacting you directly.

Contact also may not be made after the debtor notifies the collector in writing of a refusal to pay a debt or objection to the contacts; however, contact may be made to explain the possible consequences to the debtor.

Debt collectors are permitted certain limited contact with others when attempting to collect a debt. They may only contact other people to find your address, phone, number or where you work. They are usually prohibited from contacting third parties more than once. Collectors are not permitted to discuss your debt with anyone other than you, your spouse, or your attorney. They may not discuss your debt with other relatives, employers, or co-workers.

Prohibited Tactics

The law prohibits false statements, harassing, oppressing, or abusive conduct in connection with collection of a debt. This includes, but is not limited to, the following off-limits activities:

- Use or threat of violence or harm to the person, his/her reputation, or property
- Use of obscene language
- Publicizing the debt
- Repeated use of the phone to annoy someone
- Falsely claiming to be attorneys or government representatives
- Falsely claiming you have committed a crime

- Falsely claiming to be employed by a credit reporting company
- Misrepresenting the amount you owe
- Indicating that the papers they send you are legal forms when they aren't
- Indicating that the papers they send you are not legal forms when they are
- Saying that you will be arrested if you don't pay the debt
- Saying they will seize, garnish, attach, or sell your property (unless they are permitted by law to do so and they intend to take such actions)
- Collecting an additional fee not authorized by law or the terms of the debt agreement
- Communicating by postcard

Validating the Debt

Within the five days after contacting a debtor about paying a debt, the collector must send a written notice that includes the following information:

1. The amount of the debt

2. The name of the creditor who is owed the money

3. That the debt will be assumed to be valid unless disputed within thirty days

4. A statement that if the consumer notifies the debt collector in writing within the thirty-day period that the debt, or any portion thereof, is disputed, the debt collector will obtain verification of the debt or a copy of a judgment against the consumer and a copy of such verification or judgment will be mailed to the consumer by the debt collector

5. That upon request the name and address of the original creditor will be provided if it is different from the current creditor.

During a period when a debt is being verified, the collector may not attempt to obtain payment. Contact may continue during this period if you do not dispute the debt *in writing*.

Recourse against Collectors Violating the Law

You should report any collector who violates this law to your state's attorney general and to the Federal Trade Commission. You also have the right to sue a collector in state or federal court within one year from the date the law was violated.

The Original Creditor

If you are being harassed by the original creditor(s) who lent you money in the first place, you still have recourse. Different types of creditors are regulated by different governmental agencies at both state and federal levels.

No matter who the original creditor is, the first place to report the harassment is your state attorney general's office. There are a number of state laws that regulate the activities of lenders and banks. Your state attorney general's office can also direct you to another state agency if that is more appropriate for dealing with a particular creditor.

If the bank has the word *National* or *N.A.* in its title, the complaint should be sent to Comptroller of the Currency, Customer Assistance Group, 1301 McKinney Street, Suite 3710, Houston TX 77010, 1-800-613-6743.

A complaint about a state-chartered bank that is a member of the Federal Reserve System should be sent to the Board of Governors of the Federal Reserve System, Director, Division of Consumer and Community Affairs, Washington DC 20551, 1-202-452-3693.

Complaints regarding state-chartered, federally insured banks that are not members of the Federal Reserve System should be sent to the Office of Bank Customer Affairs, Federal Deposit Insurance Corporation, Washington DC 20429, 1-800-934-3342.

Complaints about federal-chartered savings banks should be sent to the Office of Thrift Supervision, Division of Consumer Affairs, Washington DC 20552, 1-800-842-6929.

Chapter 4

Dealing with Creditors and Collectors

Two very important things to keep in mind when dealing with creditors and collectors are the Golden Rule and that knowledge is power.

There are certain pieces of information that you should always keep from creditors, collection agencies and debt buyers. You should not reveal your regular phone number or your current place of employment. If possible, refrain from disclosing your current address. Never *ever* discuss your settlement account, how much you're putting away for settlements every month, how much you make, or any other information about your finances.

When you apply for credit, you give the creditor a lot of information about yourself. The lender or credit card company obtains additional information from your credit report. It may further verify the information you give it by contacting your employer, references, and so forth. All of that information is intended to be used to collect from you if you ever default on the debt. Additionally, creditors continue to gather and store information about you during your relationship with them. When you make payments, they record the name of the bank, the routing number, and the account number on the check you made the payment with. When you call in to their customer service departments, they often ask you if the address and phone numbers they have on file for you are correct.

None of the above is a problem as long as you are capable of paying your debts. However, if you've experienced a financial hardship and you can no longer make ends meet, then these things could make your efforts to get back on your feet a little more difficult. Since knowledge is power, it stands to reason that the tables can be turned by turning information into misinformation. For example, if you change your checking account to a completely different bank, your creditors' information about where you bank is now misinformation, and their power to collect is reduced to some degree.

In case you want to go all out and change your address, phone number, bank account, employer, etc., let me give you a word or two of caution. If you do all of those things and essentially cut all forms of communication from your creditors, you could create other problems for yourself. A common problem you could create is that you will not receive letters from collection agencies. You want to receive those letters. If you don't receive them, you could end up having to spend hours of your precious time tracking down who is handling your account when you're ready to settle it. Some creditors may elect to take immediate legal action as soon as they find they can no longer reach you. I recall a particular client who, while trying to settle an old account, was surprised to be told by the collection agency that it had a judgment on the account. The client had never received any legal documents concerning the account. She consulted an attorney on the matter. It turned out that the judgment was valid and enforceable in her area. She had moved and the legal documents were sent to her former address. In her state, it was considered valid for the creditor to send the legal documents to the debtor's last known address.

Here are the changes I recommend along the lines of reducing the amount of valid information your creditors have about you:

Change banks. Open a new checking account at a different bank than the one you've been using. It's best to use a smaller bank that you don't have any credit accounts with. The reason for doing this is that it makes it harder for a creditor to levy your account in the event of a judgment against you. If creditors think your account is at Bank A, account number 123456, and you've changed to Bank X, account number 987654, they would have to find the account at Bank X in order to levy it. This adds cost to their collection process and unless you owe a substantial amount of money, they are not likely to take the extra steps necessary to find out where you're banking.

Make your cell phone your main number. If you have both a home phone number and a cell phone, let your family and friends know to only call you on your cell phone. Tell them you're considering getting rid of your landline, so please use the cell phone as your primary phone number. Leave the old phone number active with voicemail or an answering machine connected to it. Use the old phone number as the only means of telephone communication to and from creditors. If you've given out your cell phone number to your creditors in the past, get a new number from your cell phone carrier (or change carriers if you want) before doing the above.

Get a landline. If you've only been using a cell phone, get a landline, make sure the number is listed so someone can get that number by dialing 411, and set it up with an answering machine. Answering machines are better than voice mail for this purpose. I'll explain why later in this chapter. Use this number only for dealing with creditors. Caller ID is a good thing to get on this phone. Then change your cell phone number and give it out only to people who need to have it. Creditors will get a disconnected notice when they call your old cell phone number, but if they call 411, they will get the new landline you've set up.

Get an answering machine/service. You do not have to answer creditor calls. They just need a valid telephone number where they can leave messages. The ability to leave you a message is very important. You should also personally record a greeting on the machine, rather than use the default pre-recorded greeting that many of today's digital answering machines come with. At the very least, this set-up gives the creditors the impression that they may be able to reach you at some point if they keep trying.

If necessary, inform creditors to call you only "at home." Creditors or collectors might call you at work. If you handle these calls properly, the first call you get at work should be the only call you get at work from that particular creditor or collector. Tell the creditor verbally that you are not allowed to receive any kinds of personal calls at work, including creditor calls. Tell them the best way to reach you is at your "home" number, which is the separate line you've set up as described above. After work, write a short letter to the creditor/collector with instructions to call your home number. Keep a copy of the letter and send the original out to the creditor by certified mail. This is more expensive than regular mail, but it is important to have proof that you mailed it and that it was delivered.

Obtain a means for recording phone conversations. There are several options here. My personal favorite is an answering machine that has the capability of recording conversations at the touch of a button. There are other devices that can be used for the same purpose. Radio Shack carries a few such devices. You can find them on the Internet or at other electronics stores. Get whichever device best meets your needs. Just make sure to have one.

You should not be taking all calls from creditors and collectors. However, when you do have a phone conversation with a creditor, it is important to record it. If you pick up the phone for some reason when a creditor calls, and it's set up to record, you can activate the recording right away. When you do so, you *must* tell the creditor that you're recording the conversation. Every phone conversation you have with a creditor or collector should be recorded. This will give you proof of any violations of the FDCPA, protect you against collectors that make promises during one call and then deny them in a subsequent call, etc. When you call a creditor or collector to negotiate a settlement, you can verify that the paperwork is accurate by playing back the recording if necessary.

Use certified mail. If you mail letters to creditors or collectors during the course of settling your debts, I recommend you mail them using certified mail with delivery confirmation. This ensures you have evidence of the date of mailing and confirmation from the post office that it was delivered and the date it was delivered. This can become important if a creditor or collector claims your letter was never received.

Getting Organized

There's quite a bit of paperwork involved in the debt settlement process. It's important. Where there is important paperwork, there should be organized files. This is a *vital* step. If you don't get your paperwork organized well, it could cost you a great deal of time or money or both.

Get a file folder and label it debt settlement. Put everything that directly pertains to settling any of your accounts in that folder. Additionally you should clip the papers for each account together. For example if you have a Citibank Visa card that you are settling, all paperwork pertaining to that card should be clipped together.

Always make sure you have paper and a pen at hand when you're playing back phone messages or phoning a creditor or collector. For phone messages, take down the name and phone number of the person who left the message as well as the name of the company and the account involved. I recommend taking these notes even if you do not intend to call the person back. The purpose of the notes is to create a trail of any account movement that may occur. In Chapter 2, I mentioned that debts can move around quite a bit after they charge off. A record of who called when can be very valuable in tracking down the right person to negotiate with. Always file the notes in your debt settlement folder after you play back your messages. Your notes will also help you detect harassing behavior by a collector. Excessive phone calls are prohibited under the Fair Debt Collection Practices Act. If you have excessive phone calls from a particular collector as shown in your notes, you should file a complaint against that collector.

You do not need to keep every monthly statement you receive in that file, though it doesn't hurt. If you decide you want to keep all monthly statements and so forth, I would suggest keeping a file folder for each individual debt you will be settling.

I also recommend getting very convenient access to a fax machine. This can be a machine at work that you can occasionally receive personal faxes on, one at home or one at a local store, such as Staples, Office Depot, and so forth. There are also online fax services that deliver faxes to your e-mail. You sign up for service and the company gives you a fax number that you can give out to other people who send you faxes. When they fax something to that number it is e-mailed to you as an attachment.

Notifying Creditors

As soon as you stop paying regularly, most of your creditors will assume that you have a financial hardship. Therefore, notifying your creditors that you have a hardship but plan to pay your debts is not strictly necessary. This is where the Golden Rule starts to come into play; treat the creditor the way you would want to be treated. In this case, I would want some kind of communication from the debtor explaining the nature of the hardship. Therefore, I recommend that you use the following creditor notification letter (which is also included in Chapter 9) to let your creditors know why you are unable to pay.

When using this letter, you want to give enough information to make it clear that you are *unable* to continue making monthly payments at this time and that is all. The example below covers loss of a job as the hardship. If you have lost income for another reason, such as illness, injury, loss of a second income in the household, or any other hardship, just edit the letter to fit your personal circumstances.

Creditor
Creditor Address
City, State Zip

Date:

Re: Account #1234 5678 9876 5432

Dear Sir or Madam,

I am writing to inform you that I am unable to continue making monthly payments on the above referenced account. I recently lost my job and am currently unemployed. I am uncertain about how long it will take me to find a new job or whether the job I find will pay as well as my last job.

I do not wish to file bankruptcy. I intend to settle all of my debts as soon as I am financially able to do so. If you have any questions I can be reached at the address below or by phone at 555-555-5555.

Sincerely,

Your Name
Address
City, State Zip

Use the phone number you have set up for creditors in the letter. Do not give them the phone number you intend to answer all the time. Do not include any specific financial information. Again, never *ever* discuss your settlement account, how much you're putting away for settlements every month, how much you make, or any other information about your finances..

Phone Contact with Creditors

While you are setting money aside for settlements, there is no reason to engage in phone contact with your creditors. This is why you set up a separate number for your regular phone calls and leave a second number for the creditors to call and leave messages. There is no need to answer the phone or return their calls no matter what they say. If you don't have funds available to settle an account, there's no reason to get into phone conversations with creditors or collectors.

If creditors or collectors start to call you at work, you should take the calls. Don't use your company's receptionist or operator or your co-workers as a buffer between you and the collection calls. It's not their job and could result in problems for you at work. When you take the call, be polite. Remember the Golden Rule. Treat collectors the way you would want them to treat you. Don't get upset with them. Never *ever* use any profanity with a creditor on the phone. Tell the caller that you cannot receive these calls at work. Give them the phone number you've set up for creditors and tell them to call you at that number. Let them know that you of course cannot answer that other number while you're at work, but they can call you after your normal work hours. Let them know any further calls from anyone in their company will be a direct violation of the FDCPA and will be reported as such. They don't expect consumers to know the law that well and will take you seriously when you cite the law.

Note: If the call is from the original creditor and the person calling you is well trained, he or she might tell you that the FDCPA doesn't apply in this situation. That is true. However that does not mean that repeated calls at work are not harassment and cannot be reported. You would simply have to report the harassment to the appropriate government authorities listed at the end of Chapter 3. Please see the sample script for creditor calls at work in Chapter 9.

If any creditor calls you at work a second time, take the call and politely ask for the company fax number and mailing address. Repeat that you cannot receive calls at work. Let creditors know that you've previously informed their company about this and you will be reporting this call and all further calls you receive as harassment. Please see the sample script in Chapter 9.

If you're being called by a collector after advising anyone from this company that you can't take calls at work and you are able to get to the FTC web site (www.ftc.gov) while working, use that site to file your complaint against the creditor as soon as you terminate the call. If you can't do it while at work, do it as soon as you can after work. If the calls are from the original creditor, make the report to the appropriate government agency as soon as you can after work. This step is very important. If you tell people you're going to report their actions as harassment, you have to follow through and make the reports. Don't engage in empty or idle threats.

You should send the following letter to any collector or creditor that calls you at work. This and other sample letters, scripts, and blank forms are also included in Chapter 9.

Creditor
Creditor Address
City, State Zip

Date:

Re: Account #1234 5678 9876 5432

Dear Sir or Madam,

I received a phone call from <Collector's Name> at work. I am not allowed to receive personal calls at work. If your representatives continue to contact me at work, I could lose my job. I can be reached at 555-555-5555. Please call me only at that number. Do not call me at work again.

Sincerely,

Your Name
Address
City, State Zip

Letters/Notices from Collection Agencies

From time to time you will receive letters from collection agencies telling you that they are now collecting on such and so account. As mentioned in Chapter 3, these letters must contain the following information: the amount of the debt they're collecting on, the creditor it is owed to, and that you have thirty days to dispute the debt or any portion of it, otherwise it will be assumed to be valid. Many people ignore these letters or throw them away and thereby miss potential settlement opportunities. If there is anything in the notification from the collector that doesn't precisely match your records for that account, you must dispute the account to the collector using the following letter. If the letter you receive from the collection agency does not include both the name of the original creditor and the original account number, *you **must** dispute the debt and demand validation.*

Collection Company
Address
City, State Zip

Date:

Re: Acct # XXXX-XXXX-XXXX-XXXX

To Whom It May Concern:

This letter is being sent to you in response to a notice sent to me on (date). Be advised that this is not a refusal to pay but a notice that your claim is disputed and validation is requested.

This is NOT a request for "verification" or proof of my mailing address but a request for VALIDATION made per the Fair Debt Collection Practices Act. I respectfully request that your offices provide me with evidence that I have any legal obligation to pay you.

Please provide me with the following:

- What the money you say I owe is for
- An explanation of how you calculated what you say I owe
- Copies of any papers that show I agreed to pay what you say I owe
- A verification or copy of any judgment if applicable
- Identification of the original creditor
- The original account number

I would also like to request, in writing, that no telephone contact be made by your offices to my place of employment. If your offices attempt telephone communication with me at work, you will be in violation of the Fair Debt Collection Practices Act. All future telephone communications with me MUST be done at 555-555-5555 or in writing and sent to the address noted in this letter.

Best Regards,

Your Signature
Your Name
Your Address
City, State Zip

As with all letters in this kit, you should edit it to fit the circumstances. For example, if the letter you received states who the original creditor was, you would not ask them to identify the original creditor. If you do not recall having a debt to the creditor they name, you should state that in the letter you send. If you feel the amount is wrong, you should add that statement to the letter. The more specific your letter is, the better. It is also vital that you send these letters out as soon as you receive the initial contact from a new collector.

It is particularly important to send out the above letter if the account number you are given does not match the account numbers you have for your accounts. I have seen circumstances where account numbers have been changed and the debt subsequently sold to two different debt buyers. By forcing the collector to verify the original account number, you can prevent double collections.

The above letter has created settlement opportunities in the past. What happened in these cases was that the collector received the validation request and responded with an offer to settle the account. In some cases the offers were very good.

Letters from attorneys should be handled exactly as above as well.

It is possible to get collectors to cease contacting you entirely. This is not advisable if you intend to settle the debt. It is very useful when the debt is disputed, and the collector continues to try to collect on a debt you don't feel is valid. In these circumstances you can send the following letter to the collector:

Creditor Name
Creditor Address
City, State Zip

Date:

Re: My ___ Account #_____ Your file #_____

Dear Sir or Madam:

With this letter I am giving your company notice to cease all communication with me in regard to the debt referenced above as per the Fair Debt Collection Practices Act (FDCPA). If you fail to heed this notice, I will file a formal complaint against you with the Federal Trade Commission and the appropriate state agency responsible for enforcing state debt collection laws.

Please give this very important matter the attention it deserves.

Sincerely,

Your Signature
Your Name
Your Address
City, State Zip

Creditors Contacting Friends, Relatives, or Neighbors

Perhaps the most difficult thing to deal with concerning creditors or collectors is their attempts to reach you via other people you know.

Most credit applications will ask you for the name, address, and phone number of someone who is likely to know how to reach you, such as a relative, friend or "personal reference." No matter how that part of the application form is worded, its purpose is to give the creditor a means of tracking you down.

It is a perfectly acceptable practice for a creditor or debt collector to contact those people in order to find out how to reach you as long as they follow the rules laid down in the FDCPA. If collector Bill Smith calls your mother's house to try to locate you (Joe Jones for this example), the following conversation is okay:

Bill: "May I speak to Joe Jones?"

Mom: "He isn't here."

Bill: "OK. This is Bill Smith and I've been trying to get a hold of him for days. What's the best way to reach him?"

Mom: "Probably on his cell phone."

Bill: "Could you give me that number? It's really important that I reach him today."

Mom: "What's it about?"

Bill: "It's an important business matter."

Mom: "OK. The number is 555-555-2222."

Bill: "Thank you very much. Good-bye."

The following conversation, though similar, would be a *violation* of the FDCPA:

Bill: "May I speak to Joe Jones?"

Mom: "He isn't here."

Bill: "OK. This is Bill Smith from Acme Collections and I've been trying to get a hold of him for days. What's the best way to reach him?"

Mom: "Probably on his cell phone."

Bill: "Could you give me that number? It's really important that I reach him today."

Mom: "What's it about?"

Bill: "He owes Bank of America $5439.32 and I'm trying to collect the debt."

The collector is not allowed to name the company he works for unless he is directly asked. He is also prohibited from discussing the debt with anyone but the debtor, the debtor's spouse, or the debtor's attorney.

You should report violations of the FDCPA regarding contact with third parties when they occur.

Keep in mind that even when the collectors follow all the rules, you may have to answer your friends' or relatives' questions about the strange call they received.

Chapter 5

Funding Settlements

The single most important factor in the success or failure of any settlement program is the availability of funds for settlements. The most common question I am asked when I explain debt settlement to people is, "If I can't pay the monthly payments on my accounts, how am I going to be able to come up with funds for settlements?" This is a good question.

Like many things in life, credit and debt are a game. The game is heavily rigged in favor of the banks and finance companies you borrow money from. The reason it's rigged that way is somewhat justified. Lenders take a risk every time they make a loan. They may not get paid back. To state the obvious, banks and finance companies have something we, the consumers, need or want quite a bit—money. They agree to lend you money by giving you a loan or a credit card if you promise to pay according to the terms they set forth in their contracts. If you don't agree, they won't give you the money—it's pretty simple. *He who has the money makes the rules.* The terms of the agreement require you to pay back a specific amount of money per month. The money you pay is divided between the interest on the money you borrowed and the principal balance on the debt. (The *principal* is the amount of money you actually borrowed or charged on your credit card.) This "game" seems to work out pretty well for you as long as you are able to make the payments. You get to buy houses, cars, and other goods and services that you would not otherwise be able to buy if you had to pay for the purchases in full with cash. It doesn't work so well for you if you can no longer afford those payments due to some life event creating a financial hardship for you.

What many people don't realize is that such a financial hardship can shift the "balance of power" as it relates to your interaction with your creditors. If you are not giving money to your creditors every month, you can start "making the rules" in that relationship. Of course the "cons" of debt settlement given in Chapter 1 have to be kept in mind, but you do have some leverage with the creditors because you are in control of when, how much, and on what terms you will pay them.

Here is how you change the rules of the game in order to settle your debts with your creditors. If you don't have access to a chunk of money you can use to negotiate settlements with your creditors, you have to put that money aside gradually until you have sufficient funds to negotiate lump sum settlements with your creditors one at a time. Let's say you owe at total of $8,000 on four credit cards, and the total of the monthly payments on those four cards add up to about $280. If you can't afford $280, but you can afford $180, you're $100 short. You can decide which creditors get paid with your $180 per month. Obviously one or more creditors are not going to get paid. You can also decide to make a different decision about your payments the following month. Maybe a creditor who got paid last month won't get paid this month. You are making the rules. The problem with playing the game this way is that you will fall further and further behind and you won't have a way out. The creditors you don't pay will add on late fees and interest and your balance will rise. You won't be accumulating any funds toward settling the debt because you're paying everything out every month. The hole you're digging will get deeper and deeper. What else can you do?

You can put that entire $180 aside every month until you can settle one account. No one gets paid every month, but your funds can accumulate to the point where you have a lump sum of money to offer to a creditor on a settlement. I recommend opening a special bank account for that purpose. Further I recommend using a different bank than the one your regular checking account is in. Ideally, the account you open will *not* come with an ATM card. The idea is that it should be inconvenient for you to spend the money that you are putting into that account. Successful debt settlement depends utterly on your ability to accumulate funds that will only be used for settlements. If you can go to your bank's Web site and transfer those funds instantly to your checking account or if you can take cash out of your settlement account at will just by going to an ATM, you are less likely to succeed at settling your debts. You should set up regularly scheduled electronic transfers from your checking account to your settlement account. Even better—if you have direct deposit, have the funds taken from your paycheck and deposited into your settlement account. It would be ideal if the account you set up for your settlement account also has a bill payment option. Again, deposits to your settlement account should be easy, while withdrawals should be inconvenient. It doesn't matter what bank you put your money in, just try to get an account with features similar to those described above.

The next question most people ask about financing settlements is, "How much money will I need per month?" This is a difficult question to answer because the answer depends on your particular situation and when you want to be out of debt. Though I can't give a specific answer, I can give a couple of methods for figuring out how much you should be putting toward your settlements per month.

You can calculate it based on how long you want the whole process to take. The first step is to figure out how long (in months) you want your entire settlement program to take. From there you can calculate how much you need to put into your settlement account each month to achieve that. The formula is this:

$$\frac{Total\,Debt \times 60\%}{Time\,to\,Complete\,(months)}$$

This calculation assumes two things. First, your balances will go up over the time you're working on settling the accounts due to interest and fees. Second, you will settle your accounts for 50 percent of the increased balance due at the time of negotiations or less. For example, if you have $8,500 in debt and you want to be done in 36 months, the calculation would go this way: $8,500 X 60% = $5,100. $5,100 ÷ 36 = $141.67. You would need to put $141.67 per month into your settlement account in order to settle your debt in 36 months. If you can't afford $141.67, then you would need to lengthen your time estimate in order to bring the required amount down to something you can afford.

You can approach the calculation from a different angle by using the amount you feel you can comfortably afford to put into your settlement account to figure out how long it will take you to settle all your debts. The formula for this is similar to the first one.

$$\frac{Total\,Debt \times 60\%}{Monthly\,Settlement\,Account\,Deposit}$$

For example, if you have $8,500 in debt and feel you can afford $125 per month, the calculation would go this way: $8,500 X 60% = $5,100. $5,100 ÷ $125 = 40.8 months. If you are comfortable with that length of time, then $125 per month is enough. If that length of time is too long for you, then you would need to figure out how to put more than $125 per month into your settlement account.

Planning Your Spending

The *surest* way to ensure that you will always have funds for your settlement account and rarely have to use those funds for any other expenses is to create a budget for your household and then stick to it. The biggest single reason for people to fail on a debt settlement program is failing to fund the program consistently. If you want to succeed with debt settlement, it is vital that you ensure that you will not spend the funds intended for settlements on other things.

Budgeting and sticking to a budget can actually be a lot of fun. It's all in how you approach the activity. Many people tend to think of restrictions when they think of a budget. I don't. I approach a budget as a tool that *helps me* pay for the things I need and want to pay for. This difference in viewpoint presents budgeting in a whole new light. When you approach budgeting this way it's best to do it in relation to your desired lifestyle and financial goals. There are some important reasons for this. The first is that you are more likely to use a budget that aligns to what you actually want to achieve. Another is that this alignment with your financial goals helps you determine for yourself what is important for you to spend money on and what isn't. If you try to budget based on my opinion or what some other financial advisor says is important or "the right way" to do it, you will almost always fail because you won't use it. Your budget has to be something you will actually *use* to succeed.

Since you're reading this kit, your priority is probably getting yourself out of debt. I will guide you through budgeting from that point of view. This budgeting guide is not meant to be followed blindly. You need to use some good judgment and adjust it to fit your own situation. Again, this is something you have to *use*, so it has to be based on your priorities and your goals. There are two fundamental rules that any budget must adhere to. *It must be realistic. It must be complete.* You might want to budget for a vacation to the South Pacific, but if you're deep in debt, I'd suggest that goal is not realistic. Similarly, if you leave something off that has to be covered, it will become an emergency expenditure at some point. These are the only things that need to be avoided when you're budgeting. Unrealistic items that for all intents and purposes are wishes and dreams and omissions of vital expenses will make your budget unworkable.

There can be a lot of work involved in putting together a budget for the first time. If you use a program like Quicken or Microsoft Money, you can create spending reports that you can review on your computer or print out. Many banks have spending reports of various types available for free as part of their online banking services. You will have a much easier time creating a budget if you can utilize these kinds of tools. If you don't have access to these things and if you don't keep very good paper records, you may have to resort to guessing about what some of your expenses actually are.

There is a complete budget form at the end of Chapter 9 of this kit, and it will be used as the framework for this chapter. You can use that form, or use a spreadsheet or a notebook or whatever you're most comfortable with. Right now we're going to go through this form section by section.

The first thing you want to fill in on a budget form is your income. We're going to use monthly take-home pay as the basis for the budget. If you get paid weekly, enter your weekly take-home pay on the Weekly Income line. If you get paid every two weeks, enter your take-home pay per paycheck on the Bi-Weekly line. If you get paid twice a month (for example, on the 1st and the 15th of each month), enter your take-home pay per paycheck on the Semi-Monthly line. Of course, if you get paid once a month, then enter your take-home pay on the Monthly line. This section of the form is shown in figure 5-1.

Monthly Net (take home) Income:	$
Semi-Monthly Income:	$
Bi-Weekly Income:	$
Weekly Income:	$
Debt Settlement Account	$

Figure 5-1. Take-Home Pay and Settlement Account

My form is set up for flexibility. If you have two incomes in your household and they are on different types of payroll schedules (such as one monthly and one weekly), each can be entered in the appropriate box.

An important point about income: If you work on commission or if your hours/overtime are not consistent, your take-home pay will vary from paycheck to paycheck. This can present a bit of a budgeting challenge. If the variable in your pay is overtime, my suggestion is to use the minimum amount of overtime you would work as the basis for your income calculations. If you work more and your income is higher, there is no problem. However, if you go the other way and budget for more overtime than you can actually count on, you will not be able to cover your entire budget when your overtime pay is lower. If you are self-employed or work on commission, the best practice is to use your average pay over a three month period.

The next thing to fill out is the amount you're going to put into your settlement account every month. You should have determined this using the formulas I gave you earlier in this chapter.

The expenses section of my budget form is designed to break down your expenses on a *per paycheck* basis. Some bills are only paid once a year, so why budget them per paycheck? You could find yourself in a little bit of a bind if you are not allocating some portion of each paycheck to the payment of those bills when they are due. If you put something out of each paycheck for those bills into your budget, you will be certain to have the funds available to pay the bill when it is due. If you don't do this, you may end up having to juggle expenses to cover the bill when it is due. This budget form is designed in such a way that it takes into account the most common expenses people have. You are not likely to have *all* of the expenses listed in the form. Just fill in the applicable spaces and leave the rest blank. In the next few pages I will take up each section of the form and discuss what it covers and give any explanations or tips I can about the items in that section. If you have additional expenses that are not listed on the form, you can use one or more of the several "Other" boxes included in the Miscellaneous section of the form.

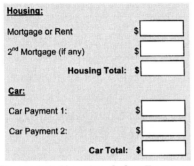

Figure 5-2. Housing & Car Expenses

The biggest section of the form is the Monthly Expenses section, because that's how we pay for the majority of our living expenses. The following few pages break down the monthly expenses by category. The categories are added up to get a monthly total and then you'll have to divide that total by the number of paychecks you usually get per month to get the per paycheck amount you'll need to budget each payday.

The first monthly expenses to take into account are the monthly costs of your residence and your car payment(s), as shown in figure 5-2.

Your rent or mortgage goes on the first line. If you own your home and you have a second mortgage or home equity line of credit, enter it in the second line.

Car payments really don't need much explanation. Enter them if you have them.

Figure 5-3. Communications Expenses

Figure 5-3 covers the various types of communications services people pay for these days. While most people have their long distance charges included in a single phone bill, it is possible to have it billed separately, so I've included a separate line for it. If yours is included in your phone bill, then don't fill in that line. Pager service is probably a bit of a 1990s holdover, but some folks may still use them, so I've left it in. If your Internet service is included with your phone bill or your cable bill, then don't enter it in its own line. The separate Internet line is for those whose ISP is not their phone or cable company.

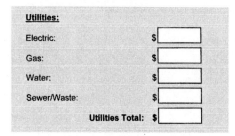

Figure 5-4. Utilities Expenses

One of the reasons these items were not included in the Utilities section of the budget form is that these services are optional for many people. A separate section for these items makes it a little easier to cut something out of the budget if you choose to do so.

Figure 5-4 is the Utilities section. Some areas, like my city, combine electricity, water, and waste removal (trash and sewer) into a single bill. If any of these services are billed together in your area, you should put the total bill in one line and leave the others blank.

Utility usage can vary depending on the seasons. Use of electricity for air-conditioning or fans goes up in the summer, as does water usage. Use of natural gas tends to rise in the winter months if your home has a gas furnace. The best way to approach this is to try to get an average of your annual usage and either set up "level billing" with your utilities so you are paying the same amount every month or simply budget for the average and set aside the extra money from the low usage months so it is available to pay the bills for the high usage months.

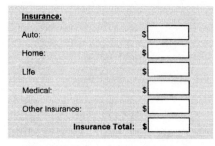

Figure 5-5. Insurance Expenses

I did not include heating oil in the Utilities section of the budget form. It is covered later.

Insurance is what I would call a "necessary evil" these days. In most areas auto insurance is compulsory. You must have it to drive a car legally. Homeowners insurance is required by mortgage lenders. Insurance expenses are shown in figure 5-5. Fill in the monthly amounts for any of the insurances you carry. If your homeowners insurance is included in your monthly mortgage payment, then don't fill in an amount for it here.

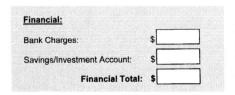

Figure 5-6. Financial Expenses

Figure 5-6 is the section for finance-related expenses, such as monthly fees charged for your bank accounts and so forth. If your bank charges you any monthly fees or if you put money into savings on a regular basis, enter those figures into the financial section of the budget form.

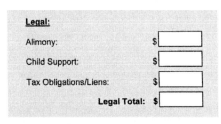

Figure 5-7. Legal Expenses

Figure 5-7 shows the section for your legal obligations. If you have monthly alimony, child support, or tax obligations you are required to pay, enter them in the legal section of the form. If you have money for these payments deducted from your paycheck either voluntarily or due to wage garnishment, do not enter them in this section. Use this section only if you have to make these payments out of your take-home pay.

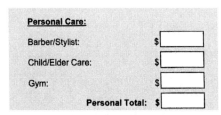

Figure 5-8. Personal Care Expenses

Figure 5-8 is Personal Care expenses. One note regarding the Personal Care section of the form: "Child/Elder Care" is different from "Child Support" obligations. "Child Care" is for day care, babysitting, or nursing home bills you may pay for your children or elderly relatives. "Child Support" in the legal section is for court-ordered payments for your child's expenses when the other parent has physical custody.

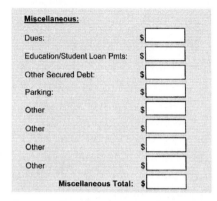

Figure 5-9. Miscellaneous Expenses

Figure 5-9 shows the "Miscellaneous" expenses. This is a catch-all for things that don't exactly fit in the other expense categories. It is also where you would add in any expenses that you may have that are not included anywhere else in the budget. I've included a couple of items in this category that didn't really fit within the other categories. "Dues" would cover any dues you might pay to any community or professional organizations you belong to, like the Rotary Club, for example. Monthly student loan payments would also go in this section, as well as payments on any other secured debt you may have in addition to a house and/or car payment. There are several lines marked "Other" for any expenses you may have that are not covered elsewhere in the form.

This was the last part of the overall Monthly Expense section. When you have filled in all of your monthly expenses, add them up and put the total in the Total Monthly Expenses box, which is shown in Figure 5-10.

If you are paid once a month, you're done with the Monthly Expenses section.

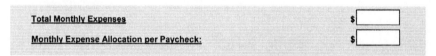

Figure 5-10. Total Monthly Expenses

If your pay schedule is twice a month (semi-monthly), bi-weekly, or weekly, there is one more step you have to take. You have to determine how much you need to put aside out of each paycheck to ensure the funds are available to pay these bills when they are due. If you're paid on a semi-monthly or bi-weekly schedule, divide the total monthly expenses figure by 2, and put that amount in the per paycheck line on the form. If you're paid weekly, divide the monthly expenses by 4, and put that amount in the per paycheck line of the form.

Quarterly/Annual Expenses:			
Home Furnishings	$	Subscriptions:	$
Heating Oil:	$	Vacation:	$
Auto License/Registration:	$	Professional/Other Licenses:	$
Total Annual Expenses:			$
Annual Expense Allocation per Paycheck			$

Figure 5-11. Quarterly Annual Expenses

Some expenses are paid seasonally or once a quarter or once a year. That's what the Quarterly/Annual Expenses section of the budget form is for as shown in figure 5-11.

Home Furnishings is generally not a regular or predictable expense, but when budgeting you should consider how often you have had to replace or repair things like toasters, microwaves, can openers, DVD players and so forth. If you've had an expense like this in the last year and you reasonably expect you might have a similar expense in the next year, then you should put a reasonable amount in the home furnishings line. My suggestion would be 1/12 of what you spent on these kinds of items over the last two years.

Heating oil is a seasonal expense, but if you budget for it a little bit out of each paycheck, it reduces the impact of the increased expenses during the cold weather months.

Professional and/or other licenses (but not for a car— we've covered that) that you need to pay would be covered in this section.

Since you're struggling and can't pay your credit cards, the only way you will be able to afford a vacation is if you put money aside for it ahead of time. You won't be able to put it on credit if you're going to settle your debts. If you want to include a vacation in your budget, figure out a realistic amount you could spend for a vacation and put that on this line. You may decide you can't afford any vacation at all until your debts are settled.

Total these quarterly/annual expenses and put that number in the total line. Next divide the total by the number of paychecks you receive each year (12, 24, 26, or 52, as appropriate).

Next we have what I call variable or irregular expenses. They are things you may have to pay some months and not others. They can vary from month to month, even if you incur them in consecutive months. Figure 5-12 shows the Variable/Irregular Expenses section of the budget form.

Variable/Irregular Expenses:

Entertainment:	$	Pet Care:	$
Clothing:	$	Hobbies:	$
Health Care:	$	Car Maintenance:	$
Gifts:	$	Home Maintenance/Repairs	$
Total Variable Expense Estimated per Year:			$
Variable Expense Allocation per Paycheck:			$

Figure 5-12. Variable/Irregular Expenses

Entertainment is a broad category that could include a night on the town, ordering a movie on "pay per view," or anything in between. This can be a wide range of activities. The reason it is in this section and not the weekly expense section of the budget is that there are various annual occasions during which you might want to spend more on entertainment than normal. Such things include birthdays, anniversaries, holidays, and so forth. My suggestion for working out how much you are likely to spend on entertainment is to start with the special occasions and figure out what you would want to spend at those times. If you know what you've spent in past years, use that figure to start with. Add in the more routine buying of CDs or MP3s, renting or buying DVDs, etc. This should give you an estimate of what you think you will spend throughout the year.

The best way I have found to work out gift expenses is to list out the names of people I usually give gifts to. I take into account birthdays, anniversaries, holidays, etc. Then I figure out about what I should spend for each one and add those figures up to get the overall number.

Maintenance and repairs for your car and/or your home are variable month to month and year to year. However, they are also somewhat predictable. Let's look at cars first. You're supposed to do oil changes, tune-ups, and other maintenance according the owner's manual for your car. You know or can figure out how many miles you drive in the average month. Hopefully, you know when you had your last oil change. With this information you should then be able to predict how much you would need to spend on oil changes over the next year. Things like tires and brakes, which must be serviced and/or replaced over longer intervals, are harder to work out. You can't predict things breaking, road hazards that damage your car, etc. It's better to make some kind of estimate on these things and plan to set some amount aside for repairs than to set aside nothing. Home maintenance and repairs aren't quite as easy to figure out as they are for your car. The basic rule here is that you will have these expenses at some point if you own your home. Again, it's better to set aside something to cover these expenses than to set aside nothing.

The other items in this category would best be described as things you spend money on when you need to. If you have an idea what you've been spending on these items, if anything, great. If not, you will have to make some kind of estimate of the amounts to put on the appropriate lines.

Total up everything in this section, then divide that number by the number of paychecks in a year, and put that figure on its line.

Weekly/Per Paycheck Expenses:

Contributions/Giving:	$_____	Spending Money:	$_____
Groceries:	$_____	Children Allowance:	$_____
Dining Out:	$_____	Cigarettes:	$_____
Gasoline:	$_____		
Total Per Paycheck			$_____

Figure 5-13. Weekly/Per Paycheck Expenses

The last section of the budget form contains items you are likely to spend money on every week or at least every paycheck. This section is shown in figure 5-13. The only items I want to cover in any detail are spending money and children's allowance. Spending money is just what it sounds like. It's a category for money you're going to spend on whatever. There's no sense pretending you won't spend money on uncategorized stuff that isn't covered in this budget (also known as impulse purchases). You will. They key is to figure out how much of that kind of spending you can afford per paycheck. That's what goes in there. It is important to give your children some kind of allowance and to use it to educate them on money and how to manage it. It should be a small amount of money that they can spend however they want to.

Figure 5-14 shows the last two lines on my budget form. They are actually the most important lines on the whole form. Add up the per paycheck expenses from each section of the form and enter that total on its line. Subtract the total expenses per paycheck from your take-home pay and enter the result on its line.

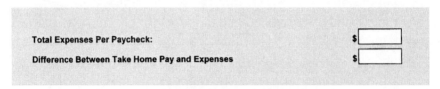

Figure 5-14. Bottom Line

It's not unusual at this stage for your expenses to be more than your paycheck. If that's the case, the next step is to try to cut back on expenses wherever you can without reducing the amount you're going to put into your settlement account. I've had clients cut out vacations, entertainment, cell phone usage, and more. One client even decided to quit smoking when he saw how much he could save on cigarettes. I cannot tell you what expenses you should cut. This is a very personal process. You simply must cut back your expenses so your expenses (including money to settle your debt) are less than your take-home pay.

If you get stuck on what expenses you should cut back on, try the following steps:

1. Make a second copy of a blank budget worksheet (available at the end of Chapter 9).

2. Mark the expenses that are matters of legal obligations or life/death (put check marks next to them, highlight them, whatever).

3. Enter the figures for just those expenses into the blank worksheet.

4. Compare your totals again. If you now have more than enough room in your budget to cover settling your debt and those expenses, you can gradually add in other expenses to the budget until you're utilizing all of your take-home pay, without going over.

It is entirely possible that after doing the above steps you found that you could actually pay your debts after making reasonable budget cuts. If that's the case, great! You don't need debt settlement! You should read the next section about implementing your budget though. It will help you ensure that what's on paper actually materializes in your bank accounts.

Implementing Your Budget Plan

Sticking to a budget is a bit of an art. How you go about it depends to a great degree on what your living situation is. If you're single, it requires some self-discipline and the system described below. If you have a partner, a spouse, or a family that will be affected by the changes you will need to make to implement your budget, you have some things to work out so that there is agreement and cooperation from everyone involved. Don't make the mistake of thinking, "I handle the finances, so I'm the only one involved." If other members of your household will be affected by your spending decisions, they're involved. If you're changing how you handle money, what you're buying, and so forth, you should at the very least make sure they understand what you're trying to accomplish. Ideally, they should be part of the team and help implement the budget plan. I suggest meeting with everyone in the household and discussing the budget and the changes that are needed. If you have young children, this is a good opportunity to teach them about money. Just keep the discussion at a level that they'll understand.

Once you have everyone on the same page, you're ready to start implementing your budget. If you've decided to cancel or cut back on some services, such as cell phone service or cable or anything else, contact those companies and get those changes implemented right away.

The items on the budget form under "Variable/Irregular Expenses" and "Weekly/Per Paycheck Expenses" are things that are usually paid for outside the home at stores, theaters, etc., while most of the other categories are bills you pay by mailing out a check or by making an online payment if you use an online bill-paying service.

There is a fun way to manage these expenses that can be very surprising in both its effectiveness and additional savings potential. It takes just a few steps, some of which you will repeat every week.

1. Get some blank envelopes without plastic windows from the local office supply store or from the stationary section of your grocery store.

2. Label a set of envelopes with the following labels, one label per envelope, using a pen or marker: Entertainment, Clothing,

Health Care, Gifts, Pet Care, Hobbies, Car Maintenance, Home Maintenance, Contributions/Giving, Groceries, Dining Out, Gasoline, Spending Money, Cigarettes. If you have children, make an allowance envelope for each of them. If you have left out any of these items from your budget as inapplicable or they were cut out, then don't make an envelope for that item.

3. Figure out how much cash you would need to cover the budgeted amount for each of these budget items.

4. Figure out how much of which denominations of bills you need (how many 20's, 10's, etc.) to get from the bank each payday so you can divide the cash into the appropriate envelopes.

5. Every payday, get the cash you need per step 4 and divide it into each of the envelopes.

6. Stop carrying credit/debit cards around with you everywhere. You have cash for your purchases as covered in your budget. That's what you spend.

7. When you make purchases that fit into these various categories use only the cash that's in that envelope. This will be difficult to do at first. You might get to the checkout at the grocery store and find you're over budget by $X dollars. Then you have a choice to make: put things back so you stay within the budget, or take the cash from another envelope to cover groceries. Though this might seem embarrassing, it forces you to think about your spending habits even more. That will result in further changes in how you handle money. You will eventually get the hang of keeping your groceries and any other purchases within your budget.

8. Work your way up to the point where you are only carrying around the envelopes you are likely to use when you go out to the store and so forth.

9. Here's where this system can become both fun and rewarding. Make it a game not to spend the cash. Each payday, put the budgeted amount of cash into the envelopes. If you haven't spent all of the money from the previous week(s), then the envelopes start getting fat with cash.

10. When you've saved a bunch of money this way, you can decide to reallocate some of the funds you've saved from your budget

to something else (like a treat for you or your family) or let it keep accumulating in case you need it for a larger unexpected expense at a later date.

I've done the above very successfully. When we first started, my wife and I had to put items back at the grocery story more than once. It was difficult and embarrassing at first, but we did it. Once we mastered that and started playing the game to have money left in the envelopes every week, we were very surprised by how much cash we were able to save over just a few months with this system.

Finding Other Ways to Fund Settlements

Up to this point I've talked about funding settlements out of your earnings from your job or business. However, there may be other sources of funds available that you might not think of using. Before I get into these suggestions, let me reiterate the disclaimer at the beginning of this kit. I am not an attorney; I am not a tax expert of any kind; I am not an investment advisor. This kit is not intended to give legal, tax, or investment advice. The information given here is meant to relate my personal experiences helping people resolve debt issues over the last ten years.

Taxes—Any tax refund you might receive can of course be utilized to settle your debt. In my experience, I have found that many people have too much money withheld from their paychecks during the year. They get big refunds every tax season, but they could be getting that money in their paychecks instead. If you regularly receive tax refunds of over $500 per year, you might consider adjusting your withholding so you get that money in your paycheck rather than giving Uncle Sam an interest-free loan. If you have a tax advisor you use regularly, go over this with him/her and get advice as to what you should put on your W-4 with your employer so you're getting as much take-home pay as possible without underpaying your taxes.

If you don't have a tax advisor, you can utilize the withholding calculator on the IRS Web site. It's important to note that the information below is accurate at the time of writing. The IRS may make significant changes to their site at any time. Those changes may make the instructions and pictures below obsolete.

The IRS has a withholding calculator on their Web site. To make use of it, you need to have your tax return from the previous year as well as your last pay stub. When you have both of those documents, sit down at your computer, open your web browser (Internet Explorer, Firefox, AOL, etc.) and go to www.irs.gov. If the site has changed, and you have difficulty getting to the withholding calculator by following these instructions, you should be able to get to it by searching "IRS withholding calculator" on Google or using another search engine.

Figure 5-15. IRS Home Page

Figure 5-15 shows what the IRS's home page looks like at the time of this writing. The link to the withholding calculator is circled in the picture.

The first page of the calculator contains the instructions for using it as seen in figure 5-16.

After you read the directions, click the **Continue to the Withholding Calculator** link (circled in the picture).

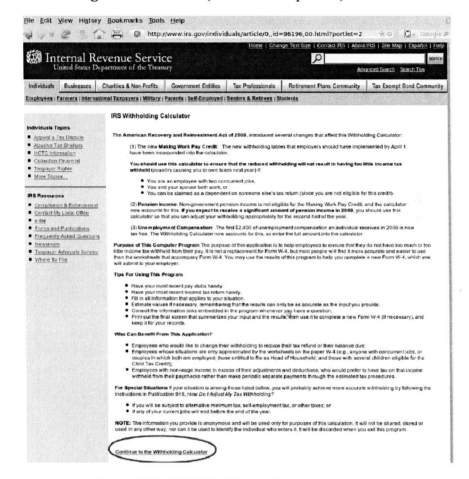

Figure 5-16. IRS Withholding Calculator Instructions

For the most part, the following screen shots from the IRS Web site are self-explanatory. Where they are not, I will give more specific instructions.

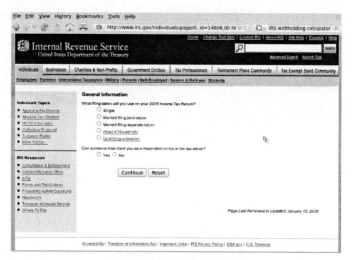

Figure 5-17. Filing Status

The screen shown in figure 5-17 asks about your filing status. Select the appropriate status on this screen and click **Continue.**

Figure 5-18 shows the second page of the withholding calculator. This page is about tax credits you may receive or qualify for. If you claimed any of these credits on your last tax return, use those figures to fill in the form on this page.

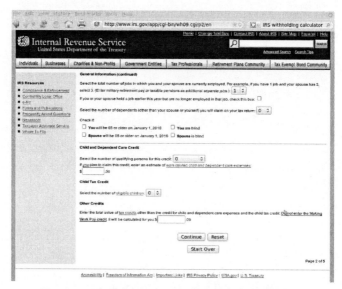

Figure 5-18. IRS Withholding Calculator Page 2

If you are not certain about whether or not you qualify for certain credits, click the links provided in each of the sections on the page to find out more information about the credits so you can determine whether or not they apply to you. Click **Continue** to move to the next page.

Page 3 of the form, shown in figure 5-19, is for your income and withholding.

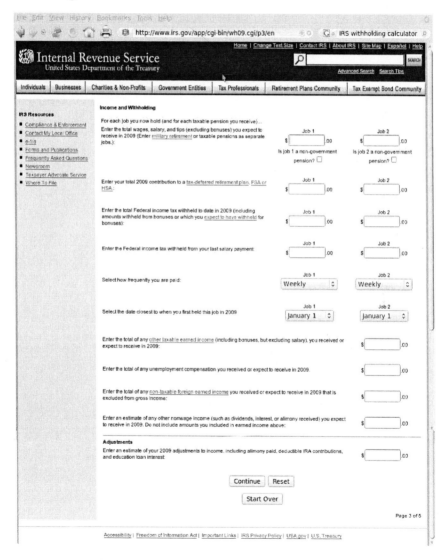

Figure 5-19. IRS Withholding Calculator Page 3

1. In the first two boxes, you can multiply your monthly income from each job by 12 and enter that number. If you get paid weekly, you can multiply your weekly gross income by 52 to get that number.

2. If contributions to a retirement plan are being deducted from your paycheck, multiply the amount deducted per pay period by the appropriate number (12, 24, 26, or 52) to arrive at the correct figures for the second line in the above form. If you put money into an IRA that doesn't come out of your paycheck, that would be entered in this box as well.

3. Enter the federal tax withheld year-to-date from your most recent pay stub from each job.

4. Enter the federal tax withheld for your last pay period per your pay stub. Change the frequency of pay as appropriate and/or the date if needed.

5. Select the date you started each job in this tax year. (If you were working at the same place(s) last year, then the date would be January 1.)

6. Use the earned income (other than salary) figure you claimed on your previous tax return to fill in the amount on that line if you expect it to be the same for this year.

7. If you received unemployment in any part of this year, enter it in the unemployment line.

8. If you have or expect to receive any non-taxable foreign earned income enter it in its line. Click on the link for the explanation of what this.

9. If you receive non-wage income and expect it to be the same this year as it was last year, enter the amount from your last tax return here.

10. Enter the amount of any adjustments based on your previous year tax return.

When you have everything filled out, click **Continue.**

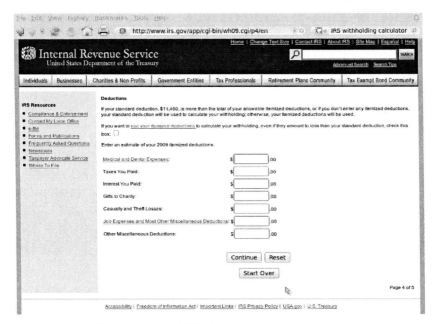

Figure 5-20. IRS Withholding Calculator Page 4

Figure 5-20 shows page 4 of the calculator. If you want to use the standard deduction, just click the **Continue** button.

If you itemized deductions and want to use those for the calculator, check the box and enter what you expect them to be for this year or use last year's figures on the above form and click **Continue.**

When you click the **Continue** button, you will be taken to the last page of the calculator. Page 5 tells you what your withholding allowances should be.

You can then print that page and take it with you to work to change your W-4 form according to the instructions, or you can download a W-4 form by clicking the link on the page and then fill it out and give it to your payroll department at work.

No matter how you fill in and submit your W-4 form, you should keep a copy of the recommendations page for your records.

Home Owners—A home may be able to be used to improve your ability to settle your debts.

First, I'll give a definition. Simply defined, equity is the difference between what an item is worth and what is currently owed on it (if anything).

Example 1: A house has a market value of $200,000. The owner owes $175,000 in mortgages on the house. The owner's equity is $25,000. At the time of this writing, many people owe more on their home loan than their home is worth. This is due to the sharp decline in real estate values in recent years.

Example 2: A car is worth $7,000 and the owner owes $8,000 on it. The owner's equity in that car is negative $1,000. He or she owes more than it's worth.

If you don't have any equity in your house, it is not a resource for settlement funds.

If you have sufficient equity in your house, you may be able to do a cash-out refinance or get a second mortgage or home equity line of credit to obtain the funds to settle your unsecured debts. There are several factors to consider here. One is the interest rates and monthly payments of the existing financing on the house. It may make sense to attempt a rate/term refinance of the house if refinancing will significantly lower your monthly house payments. This would enable you to put more money into your settlement account. There are lenders all around the country who will do this kind of refinancing if you can qualify.

It is best to do any home refinancing before you start negotiating with your creditors. There are two reasons for this. The first is that you will know exactly what you have to work with. The second is that some creditors will condition their settlements with statements like, "This settlement is void if it is paid with the proceeds of a home loan." This is silly, but they reason that if you could get cash out of your house from a refinance, they should be able to get payment in full. The flaw in that logic is the assumption that the equity in the house is sufficient to pay them and all of your other creditors. This often is not the case.

I have seen cases where home loans were made conditional upon the payment of some or all of the outstanding unsecured debt out of the proceeds of the loan. In those cases it's important to work with your lender to get the settlements negotiated while in escrow on the loan, so you can save as much as possible on your unsecured debts.

The suggestions in the rest of this chapter cover different resources that might be available to come up with chunks of cash when needed for specific settlement opportunities. Since they usually will involve some cost to you, it is important that you weigh those costs against the savings from the settlement opportunity to ensure that you would still come out ahead.

Savings and Certificates of Deposit (CDs)—Most people starting a debt settlement program have no or very little savings. However, I have spoken to people who have CDs that have not matured and they don't want to withdraw the funds early and incur the penalties. This is usually fine, but you may want to keep in mind the following: let's say you have a $2,000 CD that matures in six months. You have a settlement opportunity that would potentially save you $3,000. You're $800 short. If you pull your money out of your CD early, you might incur a penalty of a few hundred dollars (this is just a made-up example). In this kind of scenario, you may still be ahead by a couple of thousand dollars despite any early withdrawal penalty you might incur. I would not recommend early withdrawal of funds in a CD unless you had a settlement opportunity that made financial sense.

Life Insurance Cash Value—Some life insurance policies build up a cash value that their owners can borrow against. These are often referred to as whole life policies. Term life insurance does not build up cash value. The beauty of this type of asset for settlement purposes is that you usually do not have to qualify for these loans. They do not carry tough terms, and the transactions can usually be completed in a couple of days with a single phone call. If you don't know whether or not you can borrow against your insurance policy, contact your insurance agent to find out. Usually the way it works is that you call your insurance agent and ask if your life insurance policy is the kind that has cash value that can be borrowed against. If yes, ask how much is available for a loan. The terms will usually require you to make a monthly or annual interest payment on the amount borrowed. The interest rate will usually be very low. The loan can be arranged by phone and you can have your money in a few days. The one negative about this kind of a loan is that the death benefit of the insurance policy will be lowered by the amount borrowed. Still, it could be a very viable means of rapidly raising funds for a settlement. Once your debts are settled you can repay the insurance loan and restore the full benefit of the policy.

Stocks, Bonds, Mutual Funds—If these are not held in retirement accounts (see below), it may make sense to liquidate these investments to raise money for settlements. This kit is not about investment advice; it's about debt. You should speak to a financial advisor about the pros and cons of this strategy. If you pull your money out of stocks or mutual funds, you could lose money on the investment. However, as with the above sources of funds, the negatives associated with liquidating these assets should be weighed against the positives of being able to get debt settled. If you save more on settling the debt than you lose on liquidating your investments, that could still be a good deal for you overall.

Company Retirement Plans, Private Retirement Accounts, IRAs—There may be various ways to utilize these kinds of assets for settlements. Some plans allow you to borrow against them with little or no interest or penalties. Some do not. With some funds, the only way to get money out of them is to withdraw the funds early. However, because there are various penalties for withdrawing money from these kinds of accounts prior to retirement as well as tax consequences for doing so, you must consult your financial advisor, tax advisor, and/or plan administrator and compare the amount of money you could lose in penalties, etc., against the potential savings from the settlements. I have personally liquidated my IRA in order to settle a debt. For me, at that time, it made financial sense to do so. It may or may not make sense for you. Talk to your financial planner, tax advisor, etc., and decide for yourself.

Other Equity—The most common items in this category will be vehicles, time-shares, and other real estate you might have a stake in other than your primary residence (such as a vacation home or a property that you rent out). Vehicles may include your car and your spouse's car. You may have "non-essential" vehicles such as dirt bikes, RVs, etc. You may be able to liquidate these assets and use the resulting money for settlements. They can be somewhat difficult to liquidate though. They're even more difficult to get rid of if you're still making payments on them. If you have any of these kinds of assets you would like to sell, eBay is the first place I would go to try to sell them. There are other ways of selling assets like this, but in my opinion, eBay is the easiest.

Collectibles—In this category are things like stamps, coins, sports memorabilia, comic books, etc. If you've got collections like the above, you probably have a bit of an emotional reaction at the thought of selling them to pay debts. If you do, and you can't bring yourself to part with your collection, that's fine. Use the rest of the techniques I've described in this chapter to fund your settlements. On the other hand, you may be perfectly willing to part with these items. In that case, get them appraised, sell them, and use the funds to settle your debts. If you're sufficiently knowledgeable about the value of your collection, you can skip the appraisal step.

Chapter 6

Lawsuits and Arbitration

Creditors have the right to sue you to collect their debts. Each creditor agency has its own rules and policies as to whether or not it will file a lawsuit, and these policies seem to change fairly often. No one can predict whether or not you will actually get sued, but it is a possibility.

The only sure way to prevent a creditor from suing is to settle the account before the creditor decides to take legal action. You can speed up the settlement process by increasing the monthly amount you are putting into your settlement account or by finding alternative sources of funds. Such alternative sources can be family, friends, or any of the resources listed in Chapter 5, Funding Settlements.

Some credit card companies have inserted mandatory arbitration clauses into their cardholder agreements. If one of your accounts contains such a clause, the creditor will not file a lawsuit. Instead they will file an arbitration claim, usually with the National Arbitration Forum.

If you are sued or taken to arbitration, it is important you get legal advice and follow it concerning how to respond to the claims in

If you are sued or taken to arbitration, it is important you get legal advice and follow it concerning how to respond to the statements in the court complaint or arbitration claim.

the court complaint or arbitration claim. In my experience, any time a defendant (known as a *respondent* in arbitration) failed to respond correctly to a lawsuit, a judgment was automatically entered for the creditor. This is known as a default judgment. There are several ways to obtain legal advice in these matters. You can hire an attorney and pay the normal fees. Your community may have some kind of free legal aid service you can go to for help. If you are a member of a legal membership organization where you pay a monthly fee and in exchange get a certain amount of legal assistance at no additional charge, you can use that. The most well-known service of this type is Pre-Paid Legal Services®, Inc. The service I most often recommend to people is Legal Advice Line. All of its information is available on its Web site at www.legaladviceline.com.

There are a few things you should always ask when you are getting a legal consultation concerning a creditor suit or arbitration. Don't make the mistake of looking this kind of thing up on the Internet. Most of what you will find will be of a general nature. Laws vary from state to state and you must ensure you get accurate answers that pertain to your exact situation.

- Can your wages or your spouse's wages be garnished? Are there any exemptions to garnishment?

- Can they take the money in your bank account(s)?

- What other actions can they take to enforce a judgment?

- How do you protect yourself in this legal activity?

- What do you need to do with the legal documents you received?

- Is there any way to buy time or slow down the legal process and delay a judgment from being made?

The last two questions above are probably the most important questions. You need to know the proper response to make and how to file it with the court or the arbitration forum. Ideally you should get some help preparing the documents from whoever is giving you the advice. The reason for trying to slow down the legal process or otherwise buy time is to try to put together sufficient funds for a settlement before a judgment is rendered. The more time you can buy, the more likely it is you can avoid a judgment by reaching a settlement.

Though unusual, creditor lawsuits are sometimes dismissed by the court at the time of the hearing. Sometimes this happens just because the debtor shows up and the creditor's attorney does not. In other cases, suits were dismissed because the creditor could not present the most basic documentation verifying the debt. I give you these examples to emphasize the importance of following through and showing up for any conferences or hearings related to the creditor's suit against you. The point is not that you are likely to have your suit dismissed. There was one incident where the court ordered a creditor to take a settlement that the debtor had offered previously and the creditor had rejected. This kind of thing is also not typical. The point is for you to show up. The only way you can get your side of the story heard is to show up. The most common result is that you will present your side of things and the court will still award the judgment to the creditor. Unless there is some kind of doubt as to whether the money is actually owed, the courts generally favor the creditors from what I have seen.

Once a creditor has obtained a judgment against you, they can pursue whatever means are available to them in your state to enforce payment. Depending on the specific laws where you live, such actions could include wage garnishment, levy of bank account(s), liens on real property you own (such as your house), and/or selling other property you may have in order to satisfy the judgment against you. This does not necessarily mean that the creditor will actually take any action at all. I have seen some creditors sit on judgments for years without taking any further action. I've also seen some creditors move very fast in their attempts to collect on judgments.

*The most important thing to keep in mind is that if you have funds available or can get them from one source or another, you can settle a debt at any point in the legal process. You should also expect to pay a higher percentage of the total balance on legal accounts, but you **can** get them settled.*

Chapter 7

Negotiating Settlements

You will negotiate your first settlement when you have accumulated enough funds in your settlement account to settle with your first creditor. You should have about 50 percent of the outstanding balance on an account before you attempt to settle it. I suggest this amount so you have some room to negotiate. Your first offer should be somewhat less than 50 percent, but you want to be able to work with a reasonable counteroffer if the creditor makes one. I also usually recommend starting with the smallest account you have. It's a little easier to start off that way.

The balance due on the creditor's books when you start negotiations may be higher than what you think it is. This may be due to interest and/or penalties added to the balance since the last statement or letter you received. This can be particularly frustrating with a smaller account. If the creditor charges $35.00 for a late fee, in addition to interest on a $350 account, the balance goes up by more than 10 percent. The balance due on an account that small could double in just a few months after you stop making payments.

Unfortunately there is no way to stop the creditors from charging interest, late fees, and/or over-limit fees to your accounts. When it comes time to negotiate a settlement, you will need to negotiate the settlement based on the balance due at the time negotiations begin. Your negotiations determine how much, if any, of the added interest and other fees you will end up paying. Most often, the amount you end up paying will be less than the balance on the account at the time your financial hardship started.

When settling a debt, there are several details that can be negotiated. The one often considered the most important is the amount of payment. However, there can be circumstances where the amount of payment is less important than how the debt is reported to the credit bureaus. I have also been involved in negotiations where it made more sense to pay a slightly larger total to the creditor in order to spread the settlement out over several months of payments. When you start negotiations, you should consider all of these details open for discussion. You are negotiating with the creditor/collector to accept some amount of money under some terms and conditions as *full satisfaction of the debt*. If the creditor does not agree to that *in writing*, then any payment you make can simply be applied to the balance and he or she can continue collecting on the rest. It is very important that you make clear during the negotiations that you will not make payment over the phone. You will mail a check or money order. Make sure the due date for the payment allows sufficient time for your payment to arrive through the mail. Sometimes you may need to send the payment overnight express in order to ensure it arrives on time to the creditor.

I have an important maxim in negotiating:

you never get what you don't ask for.

I have an important maxim in negotiating: *you never get what you don't ask for*. With this maxim in mind, I would also say never be afraid to make an outrageous settlement offer. The worst thing that can happen is the collector will say no. On the other hand, the collector may just accept the "outrageous" offer and you could save a lot of money.

Negotiating is not a war or a contest that you are trying to win. It should not be treated as confrontational or adversarial. When you are negotiating, you are trying to solve a problem. In debt negotiations the problem is the amount the creditor is owed is greater than your ability to pay. Your goal is to find a solution that is acceptable to you and the creditor. That means both sides need to give a bit. You are striving for a win-win outcome.

To reiterate a very important point made in Chapter 5: never *ever* discuss your settlement account, how much you're putting away for settlements every month, how much you make, or any other information about your finances.

It is helpful to try to assume the viewpoint of the creditor. What would be acceptable to you if someone owed you that much money? How much would you be willing to bend? You can take this a step further when negotiating with someone who is an employee of a bank or collection company. He or she is just doing his/her job. The job is to get the company paid as much as possible. These employees may get commissions or bonuses based on how much money they bring in. There are certain rules they have to follow. They may have restrictions on what they are authorized to do in terms of discounting the debt. How would you approach the negotiations if that was your job? The better you are at assuming these other viewpoints, the more successful you will be in negotiating settlements on your debts.

If at any time during a negotiation you sense that the conversation is getting tense or heated, it's time to take a break. Politely end the conversation and make an appointment to reconvene at a better time.

Making a Settlement Offer

If you have been keeping a file for your debts while putting money into your settlement account, you should know whether you will need to contact the original creditor or a collector to settle your debt. If your debt is with a collector, you should find out if the collector is a collection agency or a debt buyer. In my experience, you can drive a harder bargain with debt buyers.

The easiest way to find out if the collector handling your account is a debt buyer is to ask the original creditor. Call the creditor's customer service number and tell the representative that you want to discuss the status of your account because you would like to try to settle it. You will be told that the account is with _____ (name of the collection company). At that point, you can simply ask, "Was the account sold to _____?" Usually the representative will tell you right away whether or not the account was sold.

Often when funds are available to negotiate the first settlement, there are several accounts with similar balances due. For example, you might have three accounts with balances due of $990, $1005, and $1100. In those circumstances, I would offer settlements on all three of those accounts. I would let each creditor know that the same offer is being made to two other creditors, but funds are available to settle only one of the accounts. You will settle with the creditor that accepts your offer first or presents the best counteroffer within a specific period of time. Follow the steps below to make offers on all three accounts.

The majority of debts to be settled are usually credit cards issued by large banks such as Chase, Citibank, Bank of America, and so forth. If the account you want to settle is still with the bank that issued the credit card to you, the most efficient way of getting it settled is to call the bank's customer service line. You want to get to a live person as fast as possible. Generally the best way to achieve this is to enter the account number when prompted and any other security information you're asked to punch in to your phone. When you get to the menu of "service" options, either choose the option to speak to a live person or press "0" repeatedly until your call is transferred to a live person.

Be prepared to spend a lot of time on the phone during regular business hours. Most banks' recovery departments are open only Monday through Friday from 9 AM to 5 PM local time (in their time zone). If they're on the East coast and you're on the West coast, that translates to 6 AM to 2 PM your time. Whatever the time differences are, you have to adjust your schedule if need be to be able to spend the time on the phone to settle your debt. Some collection agencies have longer hours during the week and/or have people available on the weekends. Some do not. In some cases the people in the collection agencies that have authority to settle may not be available during the extended hours or on the weekends.

You may be bounced from one area to another and then another before you reach the person who can help you settle your account. You may be told that the account was referred out to a collection agency or a debt buyer. You may have to make several phone calls before you get the right person in the right company to settle your account. These things are particularly true if you are trying to settle an old account. Debts can and do bounce from collector to collector to collector, and despite your best efforts to track these bounces in your files, you will still encounter accounts that you have to track down before you can settle them.

If you've gotten yourself set up with the ability to record phone conversations as described in Chapter 4, Dealing with Creditors and Collectors, turn on the recording function now. *Record all telephone conversations you have with creditors or collectors from this point forward.* ***Tell the bank representative that you are recording the conversation and that you want to settle your account. It is vital that you do this at the beginning of every phone call.*** Make your initial offer aggressively low, perhaps 25 percent of the balance due or less, rounded down to the nearest dollar. I sometimes round down to the nearest 5 dollars. For example, if 25 percent of the balance due is $326.78, rounding down to the nearest dollar comes out to $326, so I offer $325. The bank representative may accept your offer, give you a counteroffer of some higher amount, or just flat out reject the offer with no counteroffer of a dollar figure.

If the offer is flat-out rejected, you must ask why it was rejected. Don't argue with the bank representative. Just get the reason it was rejected, thank the bank representative for the information, and hang up. See the section regarding offers rejected by creditors for steps to take next.

If the bank representative gives you a counteroffer that is reasonable and you can afford to pay, tell the representative that you were only prepared to pay the amount you initially offered and you will have to see if you can work out a way to pay more. Let him/her know that you will call back within a specified time period (I usually say a day or two). This time frame is particularly important if you are offering the same funds to more than one creditor. If you've made offers to other creditors using the same funds, then tell the person you'll call back after you hear from the other creditor(s) and know what they're willing to do. The purpose for this is to create an opportunity for you to present a counteroffer to his or her proposed amount that is less than what was proposed. It also gives you some time to evaluate the counteroffer you were given without having the other person hanging on the phone.

Here are my general rules of thumb for what I would consider reasonable counteroffers:

- Banks and collection agencies collecting on behalf of banks— anything under 50 percent of the balance is reasonable. If the account is small, I am willing to go as high as 60 percent.

- Debt buyers—30–40 percent is reasonable. 40–50 percent is a bit high. Over 50 percent is definitely too high.

After several hours or the next day, call the bank back (making sure to record the call) and offer something less than the bank's counteroffer but more than the original offer you made. This amount is often accepted. If you have an offer from another creditor that is better (as a percent of the debt amount) than the one you have from the creditor you're on the phone with, say, "_____ was able to go down to X percent. Can you do that? I'm considering taking their offer and settling this account next time I have some money." This will often result in the creditor coming down on the settlement amount.

Representatives may say that they are not allowed to go below some set percentage of the balance, or they may say that they need to get a manager's approval. Ask if you can speak to the manager. If you get the manager on the phone, confirm that he or she can approve settlements below the other person's limit and then reiterate your terms. Often the representative will offer to get the manager's approval and call you back. If that's the case, give the representative your creditor-only phone number and end the call.

If your account has already been sold to a debt buyer, the offer should be made in writing. I have seen situations where the debt buyer did not have the original creditor's account number and various other things that have caused debtors problems after the settlement was completed. For that reason it is vital to make sure all the paperwork matches up with your account information from the original creditor. If you've received letters from the debt buyer that indicate a particular collector in the firm is handling your account, fax (if you have the fax number in your records) or mail the offer to that individual's attention.

Use the following template for your written offer to a debt buyer:

Collection Company
Address
City, State Zip

Date:

Re: Original Creditor Acct # XXXX-XXXX-XXXX-XXXX, your reference #XXXXXXXXXXXX

Dear (Collector's Name),

I've experienced a financial hardship. I (fill in a brief statement about the hardship). This is why I have been unable to maintain the monthly payments on this account. I have managed to put together some funds and would like to settle this account at this time.

I am offering a settlement in the amount of $_____ to be paid on or before _____ as full settlement of this account. Your acceptance of this offer and subsequent payment will constitute an accord and satisfaction of the debt. Nothing further will be owed on this account and it will be reported as paid to the credit bureaus.

(*Include this next sentence only if it is true.*) Please note I have submitted settlement offers to other creditors as well and will complete the settlement with the first one to accept this offer or present a reasonable counteroffer.

If you have any questions, please contact me at 555-555-5555.

Sincerely,

Your Signature
Your Name
Your Address
City, State Zip

Written offers of this nature are most effective when they are faxed to the collector. It may be worth the effort to call the debt buyer's office and get a fax number you can use to send them your offer. If you don't have your own fax machine or access to one at work, fax it from an office store such as Staples, Office Depot, or Kinko's. If you can't get a fax machine to use for this, you can send your offer by mail. It's just slower. If you don't have the name of a person to send your offer to, you can send it "To Whom It May Concern". This often gets a response from a collector as well, it is just less reliable. Most often the collector will call the number you gave in your offer when it's received. Since you don't answer that phone, collectors will usually leave a message and you can call back.

Following Up on Your Offer

Most of the time, settlement offers will require follow up. The representative you spoke to may have needed to get approval but has not called back. You may have faxed or mailed an offer to a collector and not gotten a response. Whatever the reason, you will need to follow up.

Following up is much the same as making the offer. Remember to record all phone conversations. If the representative you spoke to gave you a direct number or an extension to call back on, use that when following up. With banks, it's pretty common to get an entirely different person on the phone when you call back in. That person may be able to help you. Explain that you're calling to follow up on the settlement offer you made. Briefly summarize the offer and the fact that you were told that a manager's approval was needed (or any other information you were given by the original rep). If you're following up on a faxed or mailed offer, supply the date and time the offer was sent. The person answering the phone will either be able to help you or will transfer you to someone who can (which is frequently the voice mail of the person you talked to the first time). If you get sent to voice mail, call back a little later.

If you have made simultaneous offers to two or more creditors, you must follow up on all of them. Since you're only going to complete the best settlement, you've got to have something with which to compare.

Confirming the Settlement Terms

If your offer or a counteroffer is acceptable to the creditor and to you, the exact terms and conditions must be gotten in writing on the company's letterhead. Once you have verbally come to terms on a settlement with a creditor or collector, tell that person that you need a faxed letter confirming the terms of the settlement in writing before you will make a payment. Give your fax number and ask when you can expect the fax. Bigger companies might have to have the letter generated by someone else. You can often get the fax in minutes. Some creditors will take a few hours or even a day or two to get you their letter. If you don't get the letter within the time that the representative told you it would arrive, call back and nudge it up.

IMPORTANT: Make sure that settlement letters from debt buyers include the name of the original creditor and the original account number in the letter. If you receive a letter that does not contain this information, get it corrected. Do not pay a settlement to a debt buyer unless the original creditor and account number are stated correctly in the letter.

While the creditor/collector is getting you the letter from his or her company, I advise sending your own confirmation letter using the following template.

Make sure that settlement letters from debt buyers include the name of the original creditor and the original account number on the letter.

Creditor/collector
Address
City, State Zip

Re: Account #XXXX-XXXX-XXXX-XXXX

This letter is to confirm our phone conversation on (date) concerning the settlement of the above account. You agreed to accept a payment of $_____ to be paid to your office by check or money order no later than _____ as full satisfaction of this debt.

You further agree that upon completion of this transaction you will report the account as paid to all three credit bureaus. You will confirm the completion of the transaction by letter to me stating that the account has a zero balance.

You acknowledge that this is not a renewed promise to pay but is an accord and satisfaction of the debt.

Sincerely,

Your signature
Your name
Address
City, State Zip

If you negotiated settlement payments over a few months, the exact amounts and due dates of each monthly installment should be stated in the letter.

About one in one hundred collectors will tell you that he or she cannot or will not send a letter prior to receiving a payment. When you hear that, say that you must have something in writing signed by an authorized company representative. Say you will fax something over for the collector to sign. Use the above template for this by adding a signature line and typing "Authorized signature" below the line. The collector can sign it and fax it back to you. If the person refuses to sign the letter you send, politely state that you will not settle without the getting the settlement terms in writing and end the call. Move on to another creditor at this point.

At this point, if you made simultaneous offers to two or more creditors and have not yet closed the negotiations with all of them, you should do so. The simplest thing to do is to contact the collectors whose deals you are not going to take and let them know you got a better deal from another creditor and that you will contact them to settle as soon as you can put together some more funds. If you don't want to do this by phone, a faxed note is sufficient. The main thing is to not leave them hanging.

Paying the Creditor

Never pay a settlement out of your personal checking account. Never pay a settlement by phone. I have encountered situations where payments by phone were put through twice. I have seen collectors try to get additional funds once they had the bank account information off of the check that was sent in as payment on a settlement. Though these kinds of things are uncommon, it's better to be safe than sorry. It can be extremely difficult to recover the extra funds taken by the creditor when these things happen. The best prevention is to ensure that creditors never get your account number. The most secure way of paying the creditor is to purchase a money order or cashier's check with the funds in your settlement account. You can then send that to the creditor by mail or by overnight courier, if needed.

If your settlement account has a bill-pay capability included with it, you can use that to make the creditor payment if there is sufficient time for the payment to be processed and sent to the creditor. These services usually issue payment checks from one big account, not from your personal account.

Wrapping Up

It is important that you obtain documentation from the creditor showing that the transaction is completed and that nothing further is owed on this account. If you don't receive it within thirty days after sending the payment, call the creditor or collector and the documentation be sent to you. You are not done with the settlement until you have this letter. When you receive the written confirmation that the settlement is completed and that nothing further is owed on the account, file it with your receipt from the money order or cashier's check and all of the other records pertaining to this account. If you settled with a collection agency or debt buyer, make sure the letter includes the name of the original creditor and the original account number.

This kind of record keeping is vital. Sometimes an account that you've previously settled can resurface under the strangest of circumstances. In those cases you can resolve the matter by sending copies of the settlement agreement, payment, and the confirmation letter stating that the account has been settled to whoever is trying to collect on the account. Here is a real example of how these things can occur. Several years ago Bank of America bought Fleet Bank. When they merged their computer systems, there was a "glitch," whereby thousands of accounts that were previously settled were marked as unpaid with balances due in the amount that was supposed to be forgiven by the settlement. The majority of those accounts were then sent out to collection agencies or sold to debt buyers. It was a big mess. The errors were resolved by sending the settlement documentation to the bank or the collector.

Negotiating How the Settlement Is Reported

Many creditors will not report accounts they've accepted settlements on as "paid." Instead, they will report, "Settlement accepted," "Settled for less than the full balance," or something similar. In some circumstances you may want to specifically negotiate with the creditor to get it marked paid. You may even want to negotiate with the creditor to delete the account from your credit report or to delete some or all of the derogatory information connected to the account from your credit report. It is possible to get the creditor to agree to these things. Most creditors will be willing to do these things in exchange for payment in full. Some will make these concessions and still give a small (10 to 20 percent) discount. Some will refuse to make any changes to how the account is reported to the credit bureaus. If it is important to you to get these kinds of concessions from a creditor, you should include them in your initial offer. You should also decide before you make the offer whether the report to the credit bureau is more important to you than saving money on that account. You're unlikely to get both.

Negotiating the Judgment

It is occasionally possible to negotiate the removal of a judgment. Lawyers call it "vacating the judgment." They file paperwork with the courts that essentially reverses the judgment. This kind of negotiation generally involves agreeing to pay the debt in full, plus the attorney fee and the court filing fee. If you want to negotiate this kind of settlement, you should say so when you make your offer.

Tax Implications

If you have succeeded in negotiating a settlement that involves the creditor/collector forgiving more than $600 of the debt, they are required to report the amount forgiven to the IRS as forgiveness of indebtedness income. They make these reports on IRS form 1099C. If the creditor does not have your current address on file, the 1099C will be mailed out to your old address and you may not get your copy. This doesn't mean that the creditor did not report it to the IRS.

It is possible to exclude this income from your tax return if you were insolvent at the time the account was settled. See the IRS Web site for more information on this. It is helpful to make list of all of your assets and all of your liabilities with the dollar amounts for each as of the date of settlement. This will help your tax preparer fill out the appropriate IRS forms at tax time. I always recommend using a tax professional to do your tax returns while you are working on settling your debts. It can be very costly if you get hit for extra taxes because you made a mistake on a form you are not used to filling out.

While You Are Accumulating Funds

There are several things that happen between settlements. You continue to receive communication from most creditors. Accounts can move from one collector to another. New collectors handling an account may be more aggressive in their attempts to collect than a previous collector. This may result in more frequent phone calls or letters. The account may be sent to a law firm, etc.

Sometimes you receive settlement offers from creditors in the mail. If the offer is a good one but you do not have the funds to pay it, you may still be able to take advantage of it. The first thing you should do is figure out how long it would take you to accumulate the funds to settle the account. Take their proposed settlement, subtract what you currently have in your settlement account, and divide the result by the amount of money you put into your settlement account per month. This will tell you how many months you will need to come up with enough money to accept the settlement offer.

At this point you should contact the person who sent you the offer and say that you would like to settle. This is the kind of circumstance where I tend to make my most outrageous offers. I know that the creditor will definitely settle the account. The question is, how low can I get them to go? Therefore I offer only what is available in cash in the settlement account. Sometimes that dollar figure is less than 10 percent of the balance due. This tactic has occasionally yielded settlements for 7 percent or even 5 percent of the balance due on the account. Remember: you don't get what you don't ask for. If that offer doesn't fly, let the collector know that you need some additional time to be able to put together the funds. Ask if they could extend the offer by the number of months it will take you to put the funds together. If they will not do that, ask if you could spread payment out over the same number of months. Some creditors will be more willing to take a few monthly payments than to extend the expiration date on a settlement offer. Tell creditors exactly how much you can pay per month. Don't let them dictate that to you.

You may not be able to work out an arrangement at that time. If so, tell the collector that you'll call to settle the account as soon as you can put together sufficient funds.

If a Creditor/Collector Rejects Your Offer

In the course of trying to settle your debts, you will run into instances where your offer is simply rejected. I've even had collectors laugh at offers I've made. What you have to keep in mind is that "No" today does not mean "No" tomorrow or next week or next month. I've had creditors reject a settlement offer and then call back a month or two later to settle for exactly what I offered them before.

Get as much information as you can about settlement policies from the collector when you make your offer. You may be told things like, "We never settle for less than 70 percent" or, "We can only go that low if you provide a financial statement," etc. Make notes of the information you get and put it in your file.

At this point you can move on to another creditor and try to get a settlement or you can simply wait a month or two and make a new settlement offer on the same account. If you make a new offer at a later date, start with the same offer you made before. The circumstances may have changed in the intervening time. They may now be able to accept an amount they could not accept before. They may be running some sort of special (yes, there are debt settlement sales) that is only good until the end of that month. Since you have accumulated some additional funds since your last offer, you can offer them the higher settlement, but only do so if they reject your original amount. From this point, you just follow the steps outlined above.

What If I Reject, Then Change My Mind?

I've been asked this question many times over the years. What happens if you reject a settlement offer or counteroffer from a creditor? Can you change your mind and accept it later? They're good questions.

These questions are usually asked in the context of a settlement that is reasonable and that the debtor could afford to pay. The debtor just wants to try to hold out for an even better deal. Rejecting a settlement under these circumstances carries some risk. If the creditor is giving you the best deal possible on your account and you reject it, subsequent negotiations usually will result in you paying more than if you had accepted the settlement in the first place. The balance may go up and therefore a settlement for the same relative percentage of the balance would require you to pay a larger dollar amount at that later date. If the balance due is substantial, the difference in the settlements may also be substantial. The creditor may not agree to the same settlement as was offered the first time. This will also result in you paying more than you would have if you had taken the earlier deal.

Every now and then it pays off to reject a settlement offer and wait. Unfortunately it does not pay off very often. Rarely can you get a better settlement at a later date due to the creditor having a special or something like that.

If you change your mind within a day or two of your conversation with the creditor, you can probably still get the deal even though you told them no a couple of days before. The collector may view it as part of the same negotiation because of the short intervening time period. In this case I would not tell the creditor I changed my mind. I would tell them I just figured out a way I could make their offer work for me financially and ask if the settlement was still available.

If you get a reasonable offer or counteroffer from a creditor and they won't go down any further and you can afford to pay the settlement, you should take it and settle the account. Rejecting a reasonable settlement you can afford on the hope you might get a better deal later is risky. Why chance it?

Restrictive Endorsements

A restrictive endorsement is a notation on a check that states that the check is payment in full for the debt with that creditor and that if the creditor deposits or cashes the check, the account or bill is considered satisfied.

In theory, the creditor either accepts the check and the restrictive endorsement or returns it to the debtor. In practice there is a third option: cross out the restrictive language and deposit the check anyway as a partial payment toward the balance due. It is a myth that the debt is settled if the check is cashed.

In my state—California—creditors have the right to do just that. They are not in any way bound by restrictive endorsements. Check the laws in your state and make sure that the creditor will be bound by the endorsement before attempting to use one to settle a debt. If the creditor is in another state, you might want to find out which state's rules apply—yours or theirs. Do not fall into the trap of sending the creditor a check with a restrictive endorsement without first finding out if that restrictive endorsement is enforceable.

Chapter 8

Statutes of Limitations on Debt Collection

It is fairly common knowledge that if you owe someone money and you aren't paying, they can sue you. This applies to all types of debts: credit cards, oral agreements, etc. What most people don't know is that state law sets a time limit for how long a creditor can wait before filing a lawsuit. If a creditor sues you after that time, the suit can be thrown out as being past the statute of limitations. The statute of limitations varies from state to state and for different types of debt. The types of debt covered in the statutes of limitations are generally open accounts, written contracts, oral agreements, and promissory notes

If you search the Internet on this topic, you will find several Web sites that publish a list of the statutes of limitations for each state for each type of debt. These sites don't completely agree on the statutes of limitations they report. One of the reasons these sites don't agree is the definition of an "open account." Open accounts are generally considered credit lines that can be charged up to a certain limit and paid down. Credit cards fit into that definition. Some states treat open accounts differently in their statutes and some don't. According to my research, many states treat credit cards as written contracts. If I didn't find specific reference to open accounts in state laws as having a different limitation, I assume the state treats it the same as a written contract. State legislatures are always revising laws and passing new laws. Therefore I can only say that the table I am providing in this chapter is accurate as of the time it was researched.

The disclaimer one more time: I am not an attorney. This kit is not intended as legal advice. It is based on practical experience settling debts of all kinds for clients around the country. The law may be different from state to state.

I can only provide information based on research that I have conducted. I cannot provide instructions on how that information is to be used. I cannot interpret court decisions. I have spoken to a few different attorneys on the subject of statutes of limitations. My clients have spoken to attorneys about these things as well. A wide variety of advice was given by the various attorneys. In the couple of cases where attorneys from the same state were consulted on this subject, their opinions didn't exactly match. Whether the legal people agree with this or not is interesting but not all that relevant. What is relevant is that if your state has court decisions or a ruling from a regulatory agency that interprets what the statute of limitations is for credit card debt, you need to know what they are and decide how much of the information in the rest of this chapter is applicable in your state.

Statutes of Limitations on Debt Collection				
State	Open Account	Written Contract	Oral Agreement	Promissory Note
Alabama	3	6	6	6
Alaska	6	6	6	6
Arizona	6	6	3	5
Arkansas	3	5	3	6
California	4	4	2	4
Colorado	6	6	6	6
Connecticut	6	6	3	6
Washington DC	3	3	3	3
Delaware	3	3	3	6
Florida	4	5	4	5
Georgia	6	6	4	6
Hawaii	6	6	6	6
Idaho	5	5	4	10
Illinois	5	10	5	6
Indiana	6	10	6	10
Iowa	5	10	5	5
Kansas	3	5	3	5
Kentucky	5	15	5	15
Louisiana	3	10	10	10
Maine	6	6	6	6
Maryland	3	3	3	6
Massachusetts	6	6	6	6

Statutes of Limitations on Debt Collection				
State	Open Account	Written Contract	Oral Agreement	Promissory Note
Michigan	6	6	6	6
Minnesota	6	6	6	6
Mississippi	3	3	3	3
Missouri	5	10	5	10
Montana	8	8	5	8
Nebraska	4	5	4	6
Nevada	6	6	4	3
New Hampshire	4	3	3	6
New Jersey	6	6	6	6
New Mexico	4	6	4	6
New York	6	6	6	6
North Carolina	3	3	3	5
North Dakota	6	6	6	6
Ohio	4	15	6	15
Oklahoma	5	5	3	5
Oregon	6	6	6	6
Pennsylvania	4	4	4	4
Rhode Island	10	15	15	10
South Carolina	3	3	3	3
South Dakota	6	6	6	6
Tennessee	6	6	6	6
Texas	4	4	4	4
Utah	4	6	4	6
Vermont	6	6	6	5
Virginia	5	5	3	6
Washington	6	6	3	6
West Virginia	5	10	5	6
Wisconsin	6	6	6	10
Wyoming	8	10	8	10

What these statutes of limitations mean in practical terms is that you can be sued by the original creditor or any collection agency that purchases the debt during that time period. After that, the creditor may not legally sue to collect the debt. Unfortunately, this does not prevent the suits from being filed. In the real world, there are collectors out there who will file suits after the statute of limitations in the hope that the debtor will not try to defend the suit and they will win a default judgment. This is an unethical practice. They get away with it because the majority of these suits result in default judgments because the debtors never even show up in court. If you are sued on an account you believe to be beyond the statute of limitations, it is vital that you get legal advice.

The clock starts for the statues of limitations as of the date of last activity on the account. The date of last activity is the date of the last payment or charge on the account (not including interest or fees added to the account).

Collectors can continue to write letters to you and call you in an attempt to get you to pay even after the statute of limitations has expired. The statute of limitations does not erase the debt. It simply means that the creditor or collector can no longer legally sue you.

The debts will continue to be reported on your credit report for up to seven years from the date of last activity on the account.

From a practical perspective, once a debt has gone beyond the statute of limitations, you can walk away from it if you want to. You can no longer be sued, so you can no longer be forced to pay. The debt becomes a number on someone's books and a line on your credit report that you don't really have to do anything with. It will eventually go away on its own.

Whether or not you should walk away from an account that is beyond the statute of limitations is a personal decision. The main thing to consider is how long past the statute the account will remain on your credit report. Are you comfortable with it staying there? If you are, then go ahead and walk away. Send the debt collector a cease and desist letter. What can they do to you?

If you really need/want your credit report cleared up so you can buy a car or a house, I would recommend settling the account. Otherwise, it will remain on your credit report as an unpaid debt that has charged off and gone to collection. As mentioned in Chapter 7, you can try to settle the account in order to get it off your credit report. When you do this, you really need to have your i's dotted and your t's crossed. Follow all of the steps given in Chapter 7 to the letter. Partial payments on a debt that is past the statute of limitations may change the date of last activity and reset the clock in terms of the statute of limitations and the length of time the account remains on your credit report.

Chapter 9

Sample Documents and Phone Scripts

All letter templates, as well as some sample scripts to use when phoning creditors, have been gathered into this chapter for your convenience. Each letter is on its own page(s), and you will be able to copy them as needed for your own use. Phone conversation scripts may be several pages long. Each script will start on a new page with a new heading to make it as clear as possible where one script ends and another begins.

It can be very helpful to practice the settlement scripts with a friend or relative before making your first settlement offer. If you don't want to have someone else practice with you for any reason, you should practice alone. It's very important that you are comfortable and confident on the phone during negotiations. Confidence on the phone is the second biggest factor in successful debt settlement. (The biggest factor is mentioned in Chapter 5).

At the end of this chapter is a blank copy of the budget form discussed section by section in Chapter 5. You can make a copy of this form, or use a spreadsheet or other method to work out your budget criteria. Editable versions of all of the budget form and all letters are available for download at www.thedebtsolution.com/debtsurvivalkit/forms.html.

Creditor
Creditor Address
City, State Zip

Date:

Re: Account #XXXX-XXXX-XXXX-XXXX

Dear Sir or Madam,

I am writing to inform you that I am unable to continue making monthly payments on the above referenced account. I recently lost my job and am currently unemployed. I am uncertain about how long it will take me to find a new job or whether the job I find will pay as well as my last job.

I do not wish to file bankruptcy. I intend to settle all of my debts as soon as I am financially able to do so. If you have any questions, I can be reached at the address below or by phone at 555-555-5555.

Sincerely,

Your Name
Address
City, State Zip

Creditor
Creditor Address
City, State Zip

Date:

Re: Account #XXXX-XXXX-XXXX-XXXX

Dear Sir or Madam,

I received a phone call from <collector's name> at work. I am not allowed to receive personal calls at work. If your representatives continue to contact me at work, I could lose my job. I can be reached at 555-555-5555. Please call me only at that number. Do not call me at work again.

Sincerely,

Your Name
Address
City, State Zip

Collection Company
Address
City, State Zip

Date:

Re: Acct # XXXX-XXXX-XXXX-XXXX

To Whom It May Concern:

This letter is being sent to you in response to a notice sent to me on (date). Be advised that this is not a refusal to pay but a notice that your claim is disputed and validation is requested.

This is NOT a request for "verification" or proof of my mailing address but a request for VALIDATION made per the Fair Debt Collection Practices Act. I respectfully request that your offices provide me with evidence that I have any legal obligation to pay you.

Please provide me with the following:

- What the money you say I owe is for
- An explanation of how you calculated what you say I owe
- Copies of any papers that show I agreed to pay what you say I owe
- A verification or copy of any judgment if applicable
- Identification of the original creditor
- The original account number

I would also like to request, in writing, that no telephone contact be made by your offices to my place of employment. If your offices attempt telephone communication with me at work, you will be in violation of the Fair Debt Collection Practices Act. All future telephone communications with me MUST be done at 555-555-5555 or in writing and sent to the address noted in this letter.

Best Regards,

Your Signature
Your Name
Your Address
City, State Zip

Creditor Name
Creditor Address
City, State Zip

Date:

Re: My ___ Account #_____ Your file #_____

Dear Sir or Madam:

With this letter I am giving your company notice to cease all communication with me in regard to the debt referenced above as per the Fair Debt Collection Practices Act (FDCPA). If you fail to heed this notice, I will file a formal complaint against you with the Federal Trade Commission and the appropriate state agency responsible for enforcing state debt collection laws.

Please give this very important matter the attention it deserves.

Sincerely,

Your Signature
Your Name
Your Address
City, State Zip

Collection Company
Address
City, State Zip

Date:

Re: Acct # XXXX-XXXX-XXXX-XXXX

Dear (Collector's Name),

I've experienced a financial hardship. (Fill in a brief statement about the hardship). This is why I have been unable to maintain the monthly payments on this account. I have managed to put together some funds and would like to settle this account at this time.

I am offering a settlement in the amount of $_____ to be paid on or before _____ as full settlement of this account. Your acceptance of this offer and subsequent payment will constitute an accord and satisfaction of the debt. Nothing further will be owed on this account, and it will be reported as paid to the credit bureaus.

(Include this sentence only if it is true) Please note that I have submitted settlement offers to other creditors as well and will complete the settlement with the first one to accept this offer or present a reasonable counteroffer.

If you have any questions, please contact me at 555-555-5555.

Sincerely,

Your Signature
Your Name
Your Address
City, State Zip

Creditor/collector
Address
City, State Zip

Re: Account #XXXX-XXXX-XXXX-XXXX

This letter is to confirm our phone conversation on (date) concerning the settlement of the above account. You agreed to accept a payment of $_____ to be paid to your office by check or money order no later than _____ as full satisfaction of this debt.

You further agreed that upon completion of this transaction you will report the account as paid to all three credit bureaus. You will confirm the completion of the transaction by letter to me stating that the account has a zero balance.

You acknowledge that this is not a renewed promise to pay but is an accord and satisfaction of the debt.

Sincerely,

Your signature
Your name
Address
City, State Zip

General Script for Collection Calls

Once in a while you may answer a call from a creditor. If you are not ready to negotiate a settlement with that creditor at that time, use the following script. Don't get into long phone conversations or arguments. Never use profanity in a phone conversation with a creditor. Follow the Golden Rule and treat them the way you would want to be treated. It makes a difference.

You: Hello

Collector: I need to speak to _____.

You: This is _____.

Collector: I'm calling from _____ concerning your account _____.

You: OK. I've experienced a financial hardship recently. (Give a one- or two-sentence statement of the nature of the hardship.)

Collector: When can we expect payment?

You: I don't have any funds right now. However, I do intend to settle this account as soon as I am able to. I will contact you when I have some money. Thank you for calling. Good-bye.

(Hang up the phone.)

Though it may seem rude to abruptly hang up the phone, it is important that you do so. Further conversation when you are not in a position to settle the account is unproductive. The collector's job is to get money out of you. Collectors will also try to get information that they can use to collect the debt. Never *ever* discuss your settlement account, how much you're putting away for settlements every month, how much you make, or any other information about your finances. The best way to avoid these kinds of discussions is to stick to the above script and hang up the phone.

The collector may call you back immediately after you hang up the phone. At that point, let the call go to the answering machine or voice mail.

Script for Collection Calls at Work

If you start getting collection calls at work, it is important that you take the calls and use the following script exactly.

You: Hello

Collector: Is this _____?

You: Yes, it is. How can I help you?

Collector: I'm calling from _____ concerning your account _____.

You: I see. I cannot receive personal calls at work. This is a personal call. You can call me at my home number, which is 555-555-5555. (The number you use for creditor calls.) I can discuss this outside of work. Please don't call me at work again. It could cost me my job.

Collector: When can we expect payment?

You: As I said, please call me on my home phone, which is 555-555-5555. Thank you. Good-bye.

(Hang up the phone.)

Settlement Offer Script #1

Use this script when calling to make a settlement offer. There are various directions the conversation can take, and it's impossible to cover all of them in a sample script. This script covers only the most likely elements of the conversation. This script and Settlement Offer Script #2 begin after the representative comes on the line and asks any security questions he/she is required to ask to confirm your identity.

You: I'm calling to offer a settlement on my account. This call is being recorded. (You *must* say this right at the beginning of any call you are recording.) Can you tell me your full name?

(Note: Over 99 percent of the companies you call will have a recorded message saying your calls will be monitored and/or recorded. Therefore, there should be no objection to you recording the call at your end. If there is an objection, point out that the company is monitoring or recording its calls and make it very clear you will record the call.)

Collector: My name is _____.

You: I would like to offer $____ to settle this account.

Collector: Will you be able to make the payment on the settlement today over the phone?

You: No, I do not make payments over the phone. I will send you a money order or cashier's check once we have finalized the terms of the settlement.

Collector: OK, you're offering $____ as settlement on the account. How soon can you get the payment to us?

You: I can put it in the mail within two days of receiving written confirmation of the terms of the settlement from you. How soon can you fax me a letter?

Collector: I can get it to you within one business day, but I have to have payment by the end of this month, which is less than a week from now. Can you overnight the payment?

You: Yes. When you receive the payment, you'll report the account to the credit bureaus as paid, right?

Creditor: When we accept settlements on accounts, we report them to the credit bureaus as settled, not paid.

You: OK. Please fax me a letter stating all of the settlement terms we've discussed to 555-555-3333. Thank you very much.

You may be told that a manager's approval is needed or that the collection agency needs to get its client's approval on the settlement. If that's the case, you may need to follow up with the collector using script #2.

If the creditor makes a counteroffer right away, the conversation should go something like this:

You: I would like to offer $____ to settle this account.

Collector: Will you be able to make the payment on the settlement today over the phone?

You: No, I do not make payments over the phone. I will send you a money order or cashier's check once we have finalized the terms of the settlement.

Collector: Ok, how soon can you get the payment to us?

You: I can send you a cashier's check or money order in about two business days from the time the terms of the settlement are finalized.

Collector: The best settlement I can give you on this account is $YYYY, with the payment due in our office by the end of the month.

You: I see. I am prepared to pay the amount I offered. I'm going to have to try to re-work things to see if I can make this fit. I'll call you back tomorrow or the next day if I can do it.

Collector: OK.

When you're ready to call back, proceed with script #2.

If your settlement offer is rejected by the collector, there really isn't any way to script the questions you should ask other than your first question. The first question you should ask is a polite "May I ask why you won't settle?" From that point forward, ask whatever questions you feel you need to ask to get a complete understanding of that creditor's policies regarding debt settlement. Take good notes. You can then plan to make your next settlement offer in such a way that it will be accepted, or you can decide to wait to settle that particular account until another collector takes it over.

Settlement Offer Script #2

Use the following script when following up on a settlement offer you have already made either in writing or by phone.

If you made your offer by phone, you want to try to get the same person you already spoke to about the settlement.

You: Hello. My name is _____ and I am recording this call. May I speak to _____?

You will either be transferred to the person you need, or the person who answered will tell you he or she can help you.

You: I'm calling on a recorded line to follow up on the settlement I offered on my account on _____ (date). I was told that approval was needed on the settlement. Can you tell me if it has been approved?

Sometimes the person who said he or she can help you realizes that that won't work at this point and tries to transfer you. The collector may be able to look up the information in the computer and help you. If there is no further information, ask when you should call back.

If it's approved, say this:

You: Thank you. Can you fax me a letter confirming the terms of the settlement?

Collector: Will you be able to make the payment over the phone?

You: No I don't make payments over the phone. I will send a check or money order to you.

Collector: I see. Well it has to be in our office no later than _____. Can you send it overnight or 2nd day?

You: Yes, I can do that.

Collector: What is your fax number?

You: It's 555-555-3333. When can I expect the fax?

Collector: We should be able to get it to you tomorrow.

You: Thank you.

If your offer is not approved, politely ask if if the person can tell you why it was not approved. Ask whatever additional questions you need to ask to get a clear picture of what terms will be acceptable to the company or to their client (the original creditor). Keep good notes, and file them in your file. At this point, you can move on and settle a different account or continue accumulating funds until you are capable of meeting the company's terms.

When calling back to accept a counteroffer you got from a collector, say this:

You: Hello. My name is _____ and I am recording this call. May I speak to _____?

As stated above, you may or may not get the exact person.

You: I spoke to _____ yesterday about settling my account. Is there any way you can take $ZZZZ *(this should be a slightly lower amount than the counteroffer they gave you previously)* as a settlement?

You'll get one of two possible responses:

Collector: No, I'm sorry but $YYYY is the best I can do.

Or

Collector: Yes, I could settle it for that.

You: OK. I can squeeze that out. When you receive the payment, you'll report the account to the credit bureaus as paid, right?

Collector: When we accept settlements on accounts, we report them to the credit bureaus as settled, not paid.

You: OK. Please fax me a letter stating all of the settlement terms we've discussed to 555-555-3333. Thank you very much.

Settlement Offer Script #3

If you made an offer in writing but haven't spoken to anyone about the offer yet, use the following script. Ask for the person you directed the offer to or ask who can help you with it. If you sent it "To Whom It May Concern," you may hear that the offer was not received. If so, the call would go as follows. Again, it is very important that you state at the beginning of the conversation that you are recording the call.

You: I faxed (or mailed) an offer to you on _____ (date) offering to settle my account for $____. I'd like to discuss the settlement, please.

Collector: I don't have any record of it coming in. Can your resend your fax?

You: I can do that, but can you discuss a settlement of $_____ on this account now?

Collector: Yes.

From this point the call proceeds as per script #1.

Collector: Will you be able to make the payment on the settlement today over the phone?

You: No, I do not make payments over the phone. I will send you a money order or cashier's check once we have finalized the terms of the settlement.

Collector: OK. You're offering $____ as settlement on the account. How soon can you get the payment to us?

You: I can put it in the mail within two days of receiving written confirmation of the terms of the settlement from you. How soon can you fax me a letter?

Collector: I can get it to you within one business day, but I have to have payment by the end of this month, which is less than a week from now. Can you overnight the payment?

You: Yes. When you receive the payment, you'll report the account to the credit bureaus as paid, right?

Creditor: When we accept settlements on accounts, we report them to the credit bureaus as settled, not paid.

You: OK. Please fax me a letter stating all of the settlement terms we've discussed to 555-555-3333. Thank you very much.

If they have the offer in hand, the call could go something like this:

You: I faxed (or mailed) an offer to you on _____ (date), offering to settle my account for $____. I'd like to discuss the settlement, please.

Collector: Yes, I received your offer. Will you be able to make the payment on the settlement today over the phone?

From this point the call proceeds as per script #1:

You: No, I do not make payments over the phone. I will send you a money order or cashier's check once we have finalized the terms of the settlement.

Collector: OK. You're offering $____ as settlement on the account. How soon can you get the payment to us?

You: I can put it in the mail within two days of receiving written confirmation of the terms of the settlement from you. How soon can you fax me a letter?

Collector: I can get it to you within one business day, but I have to have payment by the end of this month, which is less than a week from now. Can you overnight the payment?

You: Yes. When you receive the payment, you'll report the account to the credit bureaus as paid, right?

Creditor: When we accept settlements on accounts we report them to the credit bureaus as settled, not paid.

You: OK. Please fax me a letter stating all of the settlement terms we've discussed to 555-555-3333. Thank you very much.

Your offer may be rejected or you may get a counteroffer. You deal with those things the same way they are dealt with in script #1.

Settlement Offer Script #4

Use this script when you want to negotiate how the creditor or collector reports your account to the credit bureaus. When doing this type of negotiation you have three possible outcomes: the account gets deleted from your credit report, the account is reported as paid instead of settled, or there is no change in how the account is reported. Usually creditors or collectors will demand payment in full in exchange for deletion of the account. However, you should not offer that up front. You should try to get a discount and deletion. You negotiate for a report of paid in conjunction with a discount, usually after a creditor has refused to delete the account. If you are working with a debt buyer they will be able to delete information they have reported to the credit bureaus but they will not be able to delete information the original creditor reported. If your account is with a debt buyer, skip the deletion part of this script and go straight to the section on negotiating for a report of paid, and a discount.

I don't usually recommend paying in full in order to get the account reported as paid rather than settled. That kind of deal is not usually worth the extra money.

You: I'm calling to offer a settlement on my account. This call is being recorded. (You *must* say this right at the beginning of any call you are recording.) Can you tell me your full name?

(Note: Over 99 percent of the companies you call will have a recorded message saying your calls will be monitored and/or recorded. Therefore, there should be no objection to you recording the call at your end. If there is an objection, point out that the company is monitoring or recording its calls and make it very clear you will record the call.)

Collector: My name is _____.

You: I would like to offer $____ to settle this account and have all derogatory information about it removed from my credit report.

Collector: You want us to take XX percent off the balance and delete the account from your credit report?

You: That's right.

Collector: I'm sorry, I can't do that.

You: OK. I would like to try to get this derogatory account deleted from my credit report if possible. What do you need in terms of payment for that to occur?

Collector: Well, generally we don't delete accounts, but if you're able to pay the account in full, I could try to get a manager's approval on the deletion.

(Note: If your goal is to get the most favorable report to the credit bureaus, such as deleting the derogatory account, it is to your benefit to commit to payment in full on the spot. The worst possible outcome if you do so is that you pay the account in full and it is reported as paid. This is still better than having it reported as settled. However, do not commit to payment in full if the collector does not express some willingness to cooperate and delete the account.)

You: I can put together the additional funds to pay it in full. Can you get the management approval on deleting while I'm on the phone?

Collector: No, I'll have to submit something in writing. It will take one to two business days. What number can I call you on when I have an answer?

You: 555-555-5555 *(your creditor number)*

From this point you would proceed with script number two when following up on this offer. If it is possible to get approval while you're on the line follow the section below.

You: I can put together the additional funds to pay it in full. Can you get the management approval on deleting while I'm on the phone?

Collector: I'll try. Please hold. *(after returning to the phone)* Can you pay the account by phone today?

You: No, I do not make payments over the phone. I will send you a money order or cashier's check once we have finalized the terms of the settlement.

Collector: How soon can you get the payment to us?

You: I can put it in the mail within two days of receiving written confirmation of the terms of the settlement from you.

Collector: Please hold again. *(after returning to the phone)* I was able to get approval on deleting the account if you can pay the account in full by _____ (date).

You: I can do that. I just need something in writing saying the account will be deleted from my credit report if I pay by that date. How soon can you a letter to 555-555-3333?

Collector: I can get it to you within one business day.

You: Thank you.

(Note: Many creditors and collectors have firm policies against deleting derogatory information from credit reports. In these cases the best approach is to negotiate for a discount and a "paid" report to the credit bureaus. Below is a sample script showing how to approach this.

You: I'm calling to offer a settlement on my account. This call is being recorded. (You *must* say this right at the beginning of any call you are recording.) Can you tell me your full name?

Collector: My name is _____ .

You: I would like to offer $____ to settle this account and have it reported as paid to the credit bureaus.

Creditor: When we accept settlements on accounts, we report them to the credit bureaus as settled, not paid.

You: I see. Is there any way to work out a settlement and also get it reported as paid?

Collector: Well I don't have the authority to do that, but if you could pay at least $YYYY, I would be willing to ask for a manager's approval on how the account is reported.

You: I see. I'm not sure if I can swing that amount or not, can you hold while I figure out if I can swing it?

(If your phone does not have a hold feature, put the phone on the desk or table while you work it out. You should do this even if you already know you have sufficient funds to pay the requested amount. This little bit of "theater" is designed to give the collector on the phone the impression that you have to stretch to pay that amount. Depending on how much sound your phone can pick up it might be a good idea scribble a little math on some papers, or something like that as well.)

You: OK. It's a bit of a stretch but I can make that work. Can you get a manager to approve the credit reporting while I'm on the line?

Collector: No. I will have to submit something in writing.

You: How long will that take?

Collector: One to two business days. I will call you when I have an answer.

You: OK.

(Proceed with script #2 from this point.

INCOME AND EXPENSES

Monthly Net (take home) Income: $ [   ]

Semi-Monthly Income: $ [   ]

Bi-Weekly Income: $ [   ]

Weekly Income: $ [   ]

Debt Settlement Account $ [   ]

Monthly Expenses:

Housing:		**Utilities:**	
Mortgage or Rent	$ [ ]	Electric:	$ [ ]
2nd Mortgage (if any)	$ [ ]	Gas:	$ [ ]
Housing Total:	$ [ ]	Water:	$ [ ]
Car:		Sewer/Waste:	$ [ ]
Car Payment 1:	$ [ ]	**Utilities Total:**	$ [ ]
Car Payment 2:	$ [ ]	**Insurance:**	
Car Total:	$ [ ]	Auto:	$ [ ]
Communications:		Home:	$ [ ]
Home Phone:	$ [ ]	Life	$ [ ]
Cell Phone:	$ [ ]	Medical:	$ [ ]
Long Distance:	$ [ ]	Other Insurance:	$ [ ]
Pager:	$ [ ]	**Insurance Total:**	$ [ ]
Internet:	$ [ ]	**Financial:**	
Cable TV:	$ [ ]	Bank Charges:	$ [ ]
Satellite:	$ [ ]	Savings/Investment Account:	$ [ ]
Communications Total:	$ [ ]	**Financial Total:**	$ [ ]

Legal:

		Miscellaneous:	
Alimony:	$ [ ]	Dues:	$ [ ]
Child Support:	$ [ ]	Education/Student Loan Pmts:	$ [ ]
Tax Obligations/Liens:	$ [ ]	Other Secured Debt:	$ [ ]
Legal Total:	$ [ ]	Parking:	$ [ ]

Personal Care:

		Other	$ [ ]
Barber/Stylist:	$ [ ]	Other	$ [ ]
Child/Elder Care:	$ [ ]	Other	$ [ ]
Gym:	$ [ ]	Other	$ [ ]
Personal Total:	$ [ ]	**Miscellaneous Total:**	$ [ ]

Total Monthly Expenses $ [ ]

Monthly Expense Allocation per Paycheck: $ [ ]

Quarterly/Annual Expenses:

Home Furnishings	$ [ ]	Subscriptions:	$ [ ]
Heating Oil:	$ [ ]	Vacation:	$ [ ]
Auto License/Registration:	$ [ ]	Professional/Other Licenses:	$ [ ]

Total Annual Expenses: $ [ ]

Annual Expense Allocation per Paycheck $ [ ]

Variable/Irregular Expenses:

Entertainment:	$ [ ]	Pet Care:	$ [ ]
Clothing:	$ [ ]	Hobbies:	$ [ ]
Health Care:	$ [ ]	Car Maintenance:	$ [ ]
Gifts:	$ [ ]	Home Maintenance/Repairs	$ [ ]

Total Variable Expense Estimated per Year: $ [ ]

Variable Expense Allocation per Paycheck: $ [ ]

Weekly/Per Paycheck Expenses:

Contributions/Giving:	$	Spending Money:	$
Groceries:	$	Children Allowance:	$
Dining Out:	$	Cigarettes:	$
Gasoline:	$		

Total Per Paycheck $

Total Expenses Per Paycheck: $

Difference Between Take Home Pay and Expenses $

Chapter 10

Your Debts Are Settled. Now What?

If you've followed the advice I've given you about settling your debts, you will come out at the end with no unsecured debts. You may still have a car or house loan you're paying on. These are secured debts. The big question you need to answer for yourself is, "What's next?"

I can't answer this question for anyone. It's a personal question, and the answer will reflect your personal financial goals. I am going to make one very serious recommendation as to what should *not* be next. What you should *not* do is go out and get a bunch of new credit cards and go back to spending more than you make because you can "afford the payments" again. That's the kind of thinking that got you into trouble in the first place. If you go down that road again, you will eventually end up with the same result. You will at some point (maybe many years from now) find yourself in a position where you can't afford the payments anymore, and you'll have to do it all over again.

I'm not suggesting you should not try to rebuild your credit. Nor am I saying you should not open any new credit card accounts. I'm not saying credit cards are evil. I'm saying that you need to *live within your means*. Don't carry balances on your credit cards. Don't charge up your cards to cover your expenses if you experience a loss of income in the future. Borrowing money to maintain a lifestyle you cannot afford will put you back in the debt trap. Don't do it. Cut your expenses down below your income as is described in Chapter 5. That chapter should be reviewed and applied any time your income is interrupted, no matter how temporary the situation might be. Credit should be viewed as a convenience and as a way to acquire big-ticket items you would not be able to get if you tried to pay cash, such as cars and homes.

In addition to determining what your financial goals are and how you are going to get there once your unsecured debts are settled, there are several other actions I recommend.

Live Within Your Means and Save Money

If you used the budget form included in this kit and had success with it, you should continue using it. The only real change you should make is that instead of putting money aside for debt settlement, you'd be saving toward your next financial goal. Build an emergency fund or a retirement fund, make a down payment on a home, or save for whatever else you want to save for. This alone can keep you from getting into financial trouble again.

Financial planning experts recommend having an emergency fund that can cover three to six months of expenses. I might refine this rule a little. If you have been out of work for more than six months before, then you should try to build an emergency fund that could cover the longest period you've ever been unemployed.

Maintain All of the Records on Your Settled Accounts

You should have a complete record of all of the accounts you've settled in one or more files. Those records should include the following minimum records: a statement from the original creditor showing the creditor's name and original account number, the settlement letter from the creditor or collector showing the original creditor and

The only real change you should make is that instead of putting money aside for debt settlement, you're now saving toward your next financial goal.

account number along with the terms of the settlement, proof that the settlement was paid according to the terms laid out in the letter, and a letter from the creditor or collector stating that the account is settled and nothing further is owed on it.

You need to store these records safely in a place that is accessible to you because you may need them for up to seven years. Hopefully you will not need them at all. However, I have seen accounts pop up years after they were settled. Most often they show up in the form of collection letters as I described in Chapter 7. Sometimes these accounts just show up on a credit report as unpaid and you don't find out about it unless you regularly monitor your credit report or you apply for a car loan or a home loan or something like that.

If these things happen, you will need your files to resolve the matter quickly with as little hassle as possible. It can be very difficult to correct these kinds of errors without complete documentation.

Be Proactive About Your Credit Report

Obtain copies of your credit report from each of the three credit bureaus: Experian, Equifax, and Trans Union. These are available free of charge once a year at www.annualcreditreport.com. When you go to obtain your reports, the credit bureaus will try to sell you your credit score and other services. If you want them, go ahead and pay for them. However they are not relevant to the advice I'm giving here.

In a perfect world, your credit report will reflect the fact that you have now settled all of your unsecured debt, and all of those accounts would be reported with a zero balance. These accounts would still reflect that they were previously seriously past due and/or charged off and so forth. That's fine, as long as they are reported as settled or paid and show a zero balance.

Unfortunately, we don't live in a perfect world. More than half of the time, the credit reports will contain errors. The fastest and most efficient way to get these errors corrected is to send a letter to the credit bureau stating what the error is along with copies of your documentation showing that the account is settled and has a zero balance. *Never send anyone your original documents. Send copies only.* It is also advisable to send a similar letter to the creditor or collector that made the erroneous report to the credit bureau with copies of your documentation and a request that the error reported to the credit bureau be corrected. This covers all the bases.

The credit bureaus will investigate your dispute and will notify you of any action taken. Since you are sending them proof of the error, they should quickly correct the error on your credit report. From time to time it takes more than one letter to get the error corrected, but that's pretty rare when you're providing documentation. If you did not keep detailed records as I've advised in this kit, you may have to expend considerably more effort to ensure any errors on your credit report are corrected.

Taxes Related to Debt Settlement

As I mentioned earlier in this kit, there are tax consequences related to debt settlement. Creditors are required to submit a 1099C to the IRS for any portion of a debt forgiven that is more than $600. What is a 1099C? This is an IRS form used to report cancellation of debt to the IRS. Any savings over $600 realized through debt settlement may be reported by your creditors to the IRS as Discharge of Indebtedness income. The 1099C is the form used for that report. Unfortunately not every creditor submits these reports on time. Don't make the mistake of not reporting the income because you didn't receive the 1009C from the creditor. They may have filed it late. They may have mailed it to the wrong address. Your copy could have been chewed up on the automated mail sorting machines the post office uses (it happens). People I know of that did not report income from settled accounts ended up getting tax bills from the IRS two years later. Let's just say it wasn't pretty.

If you were insolvent at the time you negotiated your settlements (which I assume would be the case), you may not need to pay taxes on this income as long as your tax return includes all the required forms, particularly IRS Form 982. I am not a tax expert and the purpose of this kit is not to give tax advice. Use a professional tax preparer for every tax year in which a settlement occurred. Make sure your tax preparer has all of the information about your settlements, whether you received a 1099C or not. The tax preparer should know how to prepare your tax return to ensure you don't end up paying unnecessary taxes or incur penalties for failure to report the income on your tax return.

Rebuild Your Credit

If you have plans to purchase a new car or a home at any time in the future, it is vital that you rebuild your credit. You will qualify for better financing on these kinds of purchases if you have good credit.

Despite the claims you might see on late night TV or on the Internet, you cannot rebuild your credit overnight. It takes time. It will at the very least take several months and could take a couple of years before you have what would be considered a good credit score.

The first step of rebuilding your credit has already been discussed in this chapter—make sure your credit report is accurate. You should review the report at least once a year and immediately dispute any errors you find in the report. This is an ongoing action. Though it is possible that correcting errors on your report can raise your credit score, this action is not enough to completely rebuild credit. You have to establish a new track record of handling credit properly.

Once you know your credit report is accurate, you need to apply for credit. You still have what is generally considered to be bad credit at this point. Therefore, you are unlikely to qualify for a major credit card right away. To start with, you're more likely to get credit from a retail outlet, such as department stores and so forth. Gas companies also issue credit cards and may issue you a card even with poor credit. There are also several banks that offer secured credit cards. To get a secured credit card, you will need to deposit a sum of money into a savings account (usually a certificate of deposit account) according to the bank's requirements. The bank will then issue a credit card to you with a maximum limit that is usually a little less than the amount in the savings account. If you default on the credit card account, the bank takes the money in the savings to pay off the debt. If you maintain the account in good standing for a period of time (usually one to two years), the bank will release the savings account and convert the card from a secured card to an unsecured card.

Apply for one new credit account at a time until you have a total of four accounts. Use the cards periodically to keep them active, but do not carry balances on them. Pay them off every time the bill comes. This means you can only charge relatively small purchases on these cards. If you do this and never miss a payment, your credit score will improve in a relatively short period of time.

If you carry balances on your new credit cards and those balances get too high relative to their credit limits, you won't be doing yourself any good as far as rebuilding your credit. High balances work against you.

If you follow these basic steps, you will be financially stable, have good credit, and be well on your way to achieving any other financial goals you may have.

Good Luck!

Appendix A

The Fair Debt Collection Practices Act

The following is the full text of the law.

US Code Title 15 Chapter 41 Subchapter V—Debt Collection Practices

§ 1692 Congressional findings and declaration of purpose
§ 1692a Definitions
§ 1692b Acquisition of location information
§ 1692c Communication in connection with debt collection
§ 1692d Harassment or abuse
§ 1692e False or misleading representations
§ 1692f Unfair practices
§ 1692g Validation of debts
§ 1692h Multiple debts
§ 1692i Legal actions by debt collectors
§ 1692j Furnishing certain deceptive forms
§ 1692k Civil liability
§ 1692l Administrative enforcement
§ 1692m Reports to Congress by the Commission
§ 1692n Relation to State laws
§ 1962o Exemption for State regulation
§ 1692p Exception for certain bad check enforcement programs operated by private entities

§ 1692. Congressional findings and declaration of purpose

(a) There is abundant evidence of the use of abusive, deceptive, and unfair debt collection practices by many debt collectors. Abusive debt collection practices contribute to the number of personal bankruptcies, to marital instability, to the loss of jobs, and to invasions of individual privacy.

(b)   Existing laws and procedures for redressing these injuries are inadequate to protect consumers.

(c)   Means other than misrepresentation or other abusive debt collection practices are available for the effective collection of debts.

(d)   Abusive debt collection practices are carried on to a substantial extent in interstate commerce and through means and instrumentalities of such commerce. Even where abusive debt collection practices are purely intrastate in character, they nevertheless directly affect interstate commerce.

(e)   It is the purpose of this title to eliminate abusive debt collection practices by debt collectors, to insure that those debt collectors who refrain from using abusive debt collection practices are not competitively disadvantaged, and to promote consistent State action to protect consumers against debt collection abuses.

§ 1692a. Definitions

As used in this title—

(1)   The term "Commission" means the Federal Trade Commission.

(2)   The term "communication" means the conveying of information regarding a debt directly or indirectly to any person through any medium.

(3)   The term "consumer" means any natural person obligated or allegedly obligated to pay any debt.

(4)   The term "creditor" means any person who offers or extends credit, creating a debt or to whom a debt is owed, but such term does not include any person to the extent that he receives an assignment or transfer of a debt in default solely for the purpose of facilitating collection of such debt for another.

(5)   The term "debt" means any obligation or alleged obligation of a consumer to pay money arising out of a transaction in which the money, property, insurance, or services which are the subject of the transaction are primarily for personal,

family, or household purposes, whether or not such obligation has been reduced to judgment.

(6)   The term "debt collector" means any person who uses any instrumentality of interstate commerce or the mails in any business, the principal purpose of which is the collection of any debts, or who regularly collects or attempts to collect, directly or indirectly, debts owed or due or asserted to be owed or due another. Notwithstanding the exclusion provided by clause (F) of the last sentence of this paragraph, the term includes any creditor who, in the process of collecting his own debts, uses any name other than his own, which would indicate that a third person is collecting or attempting to collect such debts. For the purpose of section 1692f (6), such term also includes any person who uses any instrumentality of interstate commerce or the mails in any business, the principal purpose of which is the enforcement of security interests. The term does not include—

(A)   any officer or employee of a creditor while, in the name of the creditor, collecting debts for such creditor;

(B)   any person while acting as a debt collector for another person, both of whom are related by common ownership or affiliated by corporate control, if the person acting as a debt collector does so only for persons to whom it is so related or affiliated and if the principal business of such person is not the collection of debts;

(C)   any officer or employee of the United States or any State to the extent that collecting or attempting to collect any debt is in the performance of his official duties;

(D)   any person while serving or attempting to serve legal process on any other person in connection with the judicial enforcement of any debt;

(E)   any nonprofit organization which, at the request of consumers, performs bona fide consumer credit counseling and assists consumers in the liquidation of their debts by receiving payments from such consumers and distributing such amounts to creditors; and

(F)   any person collecting or attempting to collect any debt owed or due or asserted to be owed or due another to the extent such activity

    (i)   is incidental to a bona fide fiduciary obligation or a bona fide escrow arrangement;

    (ii)   concerns a debt which was originated by such person;

    (iii) concerns a debt which was not in default at the time it was obtained by such person; or

    (iv) concerns a debt obtained by such person as a secured party in a commercial credit transaction involving the creditor.

(7)   The term "location information" means a consumer's place of abode and his telephone number at such place, or his place of employment.

(8)   The term "State" means any State, territory, or possession of the United States, the District of Columbia, the Commonwealth of Puerto Rico, or any political subdivision of any of the foregoing.

§ 1692b. Acquisition of location information

Any debt collector communicating with any person other than the consumer for the purpose of acquiring location information about the consumer shall—

(1)   identify himself, state that he is confirming or correcting location information concerning the consumer, and, only if expressly requested, identify his employer;

(2)   not state that such consumer owes any debt;

(3)   not communicate with any such person more than once unless requested to do so by such person or unless the debt collector reasonably believes that the earlier response of such person is erroneous or incomplete and that such person now has correct or complete location information;

(4) not communicate by postcard;

(5) not use any language or symbol on any envelope or in the contents of any communication effected by the mails or telegram that indicates that the debt collector is in the debt collection business or that the communication relates to the collection of a debt; and

(6) after the debt collector knows the consumer is represented by an attorney with regard to the subject debt and has knowledge of, or can readily ascertain, such attorney's name and address, not communicate with any person other than that attorney, unless the attorney fails to respond within a reasonable period of time to the communication from the debt collector.

§ 1692c. Communication in connection with debt collection

(a) COMMUNICATION   WITH   THE   CONSUMER GENERALLY. Without the prior consent of the consumer given directly to the debt collector or the express permission of a court of competent jurisdiction, a debt collector may not communicate with a consumer in connection with the collection of any debt—

(1) at any unusual time or place or a time or place known or which should be known to be inconvenient to the consumer. In the absence of knowledge of circumstances to the contrary, a debt collector shall assume that the convenient time for communicating with a consumer is after 8 o'clock antimeridian and before 9 o'clock postmeridian local time at the consumer's location;

(2) if the debt collector knows the consumer is represented by an attorney with respect to such debt and has knowledge of, or can readily ascertain, such attorney's name and address, unless the attorney fails to respond within a reasonable period of time to a communication from the debt collector or unless the attorney consents to direct communication with the consumer; or

(3) at the consumer's place of employment if the debt collector knows or has reason to know that the

consumer's employer prohibits the consumer from receiving such communication.

(b)   COMMUNICATION WITH THIRD PARTIES. Except as provided in section 1692b, without the prior consent of the consumer given directly to the debt collector, or the express permission of a court of competent jurisdiction, or as reasonably necessary to effectuate a postjudgment judicial remedy, a debt collector may not communicate, in connection with the collection of any debt, with any person other than a consumer, his attorney, a consumer reporting agency if otherwise permitted by law, the creditor, the attorney of the creditor, or the attorney of the debt collector.

(c)   CEASING COMMUNICATION. If a consumer notifies a debt collector in writing that the consumer refuses to pay a debt or that the consumer wishes the debt collector to cease further communication with the consumer, the debt collector shall not communicate further with the consumer with respect to such debt, except—

(1)   to advise the consumer that the debt collector's further efforts are being terminated;

(2)   to notify the consumer that the debt collector or creditor may invoke specified remedies which are ordinarily invoked by such debt collector or creditor; or

(3)   where applicable, to notify the consumer that the debt collector or creditor intends to invoke a specified remedy.

If such notice from the consumer is made by mail, notification shall be complete upon receipt.

(d)   For the purpose of this section, the term "consumer" includes the consumer's spouse, parent (if the consumer is a minor), guardian, executor, or administrator.

§ 1692d. Harassment or abuse

A debt collector may not engage in any conduct the natural consequence of which is to harass, oppress, or abuse any person in connection with the collection of a debt. Without limiting the general application of the foregoing, the following conduct is a violation of this section:

(1) The use or threat of use of violence or other criminal means to harm the physical person, reputation, or property of any person.

(2) The use of obscene or profane language or language the natural consequence of which is to abuse the hearer or reader.

(3) The publication of a list of consumers who allegedly refuse to pay debts, except to a consumer reporting agency or to persons meeting the requirements of section 1681a (f) or 1681b (3) of this title.

(4) The advertisement for sale of any debt to coerce payment of the debt.

(5) Causing a telephone to ring or engaging any person in telephone conversation repeatedly or continuously with intent to annoy, abuse, or harass any person at the called number.

(6) Except as provided in section 1692b, the placement of telephone calls without meaningful disclosure of the caller's identity.

§ 1692e. False or misleading representations

A debt collector may not use any false, deceptive, or misleading representation or means in connection with the collection of any debt. Without limiting the general application of the foregoing, the following conduct is a violation of this section:

(1) The false representation or implication that the debt collector is vouched for, bonded by, or affiliated with the United States or any State, including the use of any badge, uniform, or facsimile thereof.

(2) The false representation of—

(A) the character, amount, or legal status of any debt; or

(B) any services rendered or compensation which may be lawfully received by any debt collector for the collection of a debt.

(3) The false representation or implication that any individual is an attorney or that any communication is from an attorney.

(4) The representation or implication that nonpayment of any debt will result in the arrest or imprisonment of any person or the seizure, garnishment, attachment, or sale of any property or wages of any person unless such action is lawful and the debt collector or creditor intends to take such action.

(5) The threat to take any action that cannot legally be taken or that is not intended to be taken.

(6) The false representation or implication that a sale, referral, or other transfer of any interest in a debt shall cause the consumer to—

(A) lose any claim or defense to payment of the debt; or

(B) become subject to any practice prohibited by this title.

(7) The false representation or implication that the consumer committed any crime or other conduct in order to disgrace the consumer.

(8) Communicating or threatening to communicate to any person credit information which is known or which should be known to be false, including the failure to communicate that a disputed debt is disputed.

(9) The use or distribution of any written communication which simulates or is falsely represented to be a document authorized, issued, or approved by any court, official, or agency of the United States or any State, or which creates a false impression as to its source, authorization, or approval.

(10) The use of any false representation or deceptive means to collect or attempt to collect any debt or to obtain information concerning a consumer.

(11) The failure to disclose in the initial written communication with the consumer and, in addition, if the initial communication with the consumer is oral, in that initial oral communication, that the debt collector is attempting to collect a debt and that any information obtained will be used for that purpose, and the failure to disclose in subsequent

communications that the communication is from a debt collector, except that this paragraph shall not apply to a formal pleading made in connection with a legal action.

(12) The false representation or implication that accounts have been turned over to innocent purchasers for value.

(13) The false representation or implication that documents are legal process.

(14) The use of any business, company, or organization name other than the true name of the debt collector's business, company, or organization.

(15) The false representation or implication that documents are not legal process forms or do not require action by the consumer.

(16) The false representation or implication that a debt collector operates or is employed by a consumer reporting agency as defined by section 1681a (f) of this title.

§ 1692f. Unfair practices

A debt collector may not use unfair or unconscionable means to collect or attempt to collect any debt. Without limiting the general application of the foregoing, the following conduct is a violation of this section:

(1) The collection of any amount (including any interest, fee, charge, or expense incidental to the principal obligation) unless such amount is expressly authorized by the agreement creating the debt or permitted by law.

(2) The acceptance by a debt collector from any person of a check or other payment instrument postdated by more than five days unless such person is notified in writing of the debt collector's intent to deposit such check or instrument not more than ten nor less than three business days prior to such deposit.

(3) The solicitation by a debt collector of any postdated check or other postdated payment instrument for the purpose of threatening or instituting criminal prosecution.

(4) Depositing or threatening to deposit any postdated check or other postdated payment instrument prior to the date on such check or instrument.

(5) Causing charges to be made to any person for communications by concealment of the true propose of the communication. Such charges include, but are not limited to, collect telephone calls and telegram fees.

(6) Taking or threatening to take any nonjudicial action to effect dispossession or disablement of property if—

    (A) there is no present right to possession of the property claimed as collateral through an enforceable security interest;

    (B) there is no present intention to take possession of the property; or

    (C) the property is exempt by law from such dispossession or disablement.

(7) Communicating with a consumer regarding a debt by post card.

(8) Using any language or symbol, other than the debt collector's address, on any envelope when communicating with a consumer by use of the mails or by telegram, except that a debt collector may use his business name if such name does not indicate that he is in the debt collection business.

§ 1692g. Validation of debts

(a) Within five days after the initial communication with a consumer in connection with the collection of any debt, a debt collector shall, unless the following information is contained in the initial communication or the consumer has paid the debt, send the consumer a written notice containing—

    (1) the amount of the debt;

    (2) the name of the creditor to whom the debt is owed;

    (3) a statement that unless the consumer, within thirty days after receipt of the notice, disputes the validity of the debt, or any portion thereof, the debt will be assumed to be valid by the debt collector;

(4)   a statement that if the consumer notifies the debt collector in writing within the thirty-day period that the debt, or any portion thereof, is disputed, the debt collector will obtain verification of the debt or a copy of a judgment against the consumer and a copy of such verification or judgment will be mailed to the consumer by the debt collector; and

(5)   a statement that, upon the consumer's written request within the thirty-day period, the debt collector will provide the consumer with the name and address of the original creditor, if different from the current creditor.

(b)   If the consumer notifies the debt collector in writing within the thirty-day period described in subsection (a) that the debt, or any portion thereof, is disputed, or that the consumer requests the name and address of the original creditor, the debt collector shall cease collection of the debt, or any disputed portion thereof, until the debt collector obtains verification of the debt or any copy of a judgment, or the name and address of the original creditor, and a copy of such verification or judgment, or name and address of the original creditor, is mailed to the consumer by the debt collector. Collection activities and communications that do not otherwise violate this title may continue during the 30-day period referred to in subsection (a) unless the consumer has notified the debt collector in writing that the debt, or any portion of the debt, is disputed or that the consumer requests the name and address of the original creditor. Any collection activities and communication during the 30-day period may not overshadow or be inconsistent with the disclosure of the consumer's right to dispute the debt or request the name and address of the original creditor.

(c)   The failure of a consumer to dispute the validity of a debt under this section may not be construed by any court as an admission of liability by the consumer.

(d)   A communication in the form of a formal pleading in a civil action shall not be treated as an initial communication for purposes of subsection (a).

(e)   The sending or delivery of any form or notice which does not relate to the collection of a debt and is expressly required by the Internal Revenue Code of 1986, title V of Gramm-Leach-Bliley Act, or any provision of Federal or State law relating to notice of data security breach or privacy, or any regulation prescribed under any such provision of law, shall not be treated as an initial communication in connection with debt collection for purposes of this section.

§ 1692h. Multiple debts

If any consumer owes multiple debts and makes any single payment to any debt collector with respect to such debts, such debt collector may not apply such payment to any debt which is disputed by the consumer and, where applicable, shall apply such   payment in accordance with the consumer's directions.

§ 1692i. Legal actions by debt collectors

(a)   Any debt collector who brings any legal action on a debt against any consumer shall—

   (1)   in the case of an action to enforce an interest in real property securing the consumer's obligation, bring such action only in a judicial district or similar legal entity in which such real property is located; or

   (2)   in the case of an action not described in paragraph (1), bring such action only in the judicial district or similar legal entity—

      (A)   in which such consumer signed the contract sued upon; or

      (B)   in which such consumer resides at the commencement of the action.

(b)   Nothing in this title shall be construed to authorize the bringing of legal actions by debt collectors.

§ 1692j. Furnishing certain deceptive forms

(a)   It is unlawful to design, compile, and furnish any form knowing that such form would be used to create the false belief in a consumer that a person other than the creditor of such consumer is participating in the collection of or in an attempt to collect a debt such consumer allegedly owes such creditor, when in fact such person is not so participating.

(b)   Any person who violates this section shall be liable to the same extent and in the same manner as a debt collector is liable under section 1692k for failure to comply with a provision of this title.

§ 1692k. Civil liability

(a)   Except as otherwise provided by this section, any debt collector who fails to comply with any provision of this title with respect to any person is liable to such person in an amount equal to the sum of—

(1)   any actual damage sustained by such person as a result of such failure;

(2)

(A)   in the case of any action by an individual, such additional damages as the court may allow, but not exceeding $1,000; or

(B)   in the case of a class action,

(i)   such amount for each named plaintiff as could be recovered under subparagraph (A), and

(ii)   such amount as the court may allow for all other class members, without regard to a minimum individual recovery, not to exceed the lesser of $500,000 or 1 per centum of the net worth of the debt collector; and

(3)   in the case of any successful action to enforce the foregoing liability, the costs of the action, together with a reasonable attorney's fee as determined by the court. On a finding by the court that an action under this section was brought in bad faith and for the purpose of harassment, the court may award to the

defendant attorney's fees reasonable in relation to the work expended and costs.

(b) In determining the amount of liability in any action under subsection (a), the court shall consider, among other relevant factors—

    (1) in any individual action under subsection (a)(2)(A), the frequency and persistence of noncompliance by the debt collector, the nature of such noncompliance, and the extent to which such noncompliance was intentional; or

    (2) in any class action under subsection (a)(2)(B), the frequency and persistence of noncompliance by the debt collector, the nature of such noncompliance, the resources of the debt collector, the number of persons adversely affected, and the extent to which the debt collector's noncompliance was intentional.

(c) A debt collector may not be held liable in any action brought under this title if the debt collector shows by a preponderance of evidence that the violation was not intentional and resulted from a bona fide error notwithstanding the maintenance of procedures reasonably adapted to avoid any such error.

(d) An action to enforce any liability created by this title may be brought in any appropriate United States district court without regard to the amount in controversy, or in any other court of competent jurisdiction, within one year from the date on which the violation occurs.

(e) No provision of this section imposing any liability shall apply to any act done or omitted in good faith in conformity with any advisory opinion of the Commission, notwithstanding that after such act or omission has occurred, such opinion is amended, rescinded, or determined by judicial or other authority to be invalid for any reason.

§ 1692l. Administrative enforcement

(a) Compliance with this title shall be enforced by the Commission, except to the extent that enforcement of the requirements imposed under this title is specifically committed to another agency under subsection (b). For purpose of the exercise by the Commission of its functions and powers under the Federal Trade Commission Act, a violation of this title shall be deemed an unfair or deceptive act or practice in violation of that Act. All of the functions and powers of the Commission under the Federal Trade Commission Act are available to the Commission to enforce compliance by any person with this title, irrespective of whether that person is engaged in commerce or meets any other jurisdictional tests in the Federal Trade Commission Act, including the power to enforce the provisions of this title in the same manner as if the violation had been a violation of a Federal Trade Commission trade regulation rule.

(b)   Compliance with any requirements imposed under this title shall be enforced under—

    (1)   section 8 of the Federal Deposit Insurance Act, in the case of—

        (A)   national banks, and Federal branches and Federal agencies of foreign banks, by the Office of the Comptroller of the Currency;

        (B)   member banks of the Federal Reserve System (other than national banks), branches and agencies of foreign banks (other than Federal branches, Federal agencies, and insured State branches of foreign banks), commercial lending companies owned or controlled by foreign banks, and organizations operating under section 25 or 25(a) of the Federal Reserve Act, by the Board of Governors of the Federal Reserve System; and

        (C)   banks insured by the Federal Deposit Insurance Corporation (other than members of the Federal Reserve System) and insured State branches of foreign banks, by the Board of Directors of the Federal Deposit Insurance Corporation;

    (2)   section 8 of the Federal Deposit Insurance Act, by the Director of the Office of Thrift Supervision, in the case

of a savings association the deposits of which are insured by the Federal Deposit Insurance Corporation;

(3)   the Federal Credit Union Act, by the Administrator of the National Credit Union Administration with respect to any Federal credit union;

(4)   the Acts to regulate commerce, by the Secretary of Transportation, with respect to all carriers subject to the jurisdiction of the Surface Transportation Board;

(5)   the Federal Aviation Act of 1958, by the Secretary of Transportation with respect to any air carrier or any foreign air carrier subject to that Act; and

(6)   the Packers and Stockyards Act, 1921 (except as provided in section 406 of that Act), by the Secretary of Agriculture with respect to any activities subject to that Act.

The terms used in paragraph (1) that are not defined in this title or otherwise defined in section 3(s) of the Federal Deposit Insurance Act (12 U.S.C. 1813(s)) shall have the meaning given to them in section 1(b) of the International Banking Act of 1978 (12 U.S.C. 3101).

(c)   For the purpose of the exercise by any agency referred to in subsection (b) of its powers under any Act referred to in that subsection, a violation of any requirement imposed under this title shall be deemed to be a violation of a requirement imposed under that Act. In addition to its powers under any provision of law specifically referred to in subsection (b), each of the agencies referred to in that subsection may exercise, for the purpose of enforcing compliance with any requirement imposed under this title any other authority conferred on it by law, except as provided in subsection (d).

(d)   Neither the Commission nor any other agency referred to in subsection (b) may promulgate trade regulation rules or other regulations with respect to the collection of debts by debt collectors as defined in this title.

§ 1692m. Reports to Congress by the Commission

(a)   Not later than one year after the effective date of this title and at one-year intervals thereafter, the Commission shall make reports to the Congress concerning the administration of its functions under this title, including such recommendations as the Commission deems necessary or appropriate. In addition, each report of the Commission shall include its assessment of the extent to which compliance with this title is being achieved and a summary of the enforcement actions taken by the Commission under section 1692l of this title.

(b)   In the exercise of its functions under this title, the Commission may obtain upon request the views of any other Federal agency which exercises enforcement functions under section 1692l of this title.

§ 1692n. Relation to State laws

This title does not annul, alter, or affect, or exempt any person subject to the provisions of this title from complying with the laws of any State with respect to debt collection practices, except to the extent that those laws are inconsistent with any provision of this title, and then only to the extent of the inconsistency. For purposes of this section, a State law is not inconsistent with this title if the protection such law affords any consumer is greater than the protection provided by this title.

§ 1692o. Exemption for State regulation

The Commission shall by regulation exempt from the requirements of this title any class of debt collection practices within any State if the Commission determines that under the law of that State that class of debt collection practices is subject to requirements substantially similar to those imposed by this title, and that there is adequate provision for enforcement.

§ 1692p. Exception for certain bad check enforcement programs operated by private entities

(a) In General—

(1) TREATMENT OF CERTAIN PRIVATE ENTITIES— Subject to paragraph (2), a private entity shall be excluded from the definition of a debt collector, pursuant to the exception provided in section 803(6), with respect to the operation by the entity of a program described in paragraph (2)(A) under a contract described in paragraph (2)(B).

(2) CONDITIONS OF APPLICABILITY—Paragraph (1) shall apply if—

(A) a State or district attorney establishes, within the jurisdiction of such State or district attorney and with respect to alleged bad check violations that do not involve a check described in subsection (b), a pretrial diversion program for alleged bad check offenders who agree to participate voluntarily in such program to avoid criminal prosecution;

(B) a private entity, that is subject to an administrative support services contract with a State or district attorney and operates under the direction, supervision, and control of such State or district attorney, operates the pretrial diversion program described in subparagraph (A); and

(C) in the course of performing duties delegated to it by a State or district attorney under the contract, the private entity referred to in subparagraph (B)—

(i) complies with the penal laws of the State;

(ii) conforms with the terms of the contract and directives of the State or district attorney;

(iii) does not exercise independent prosecutorial discretion;

(iv) contacts any alleged offender referred to in subparagraph (A) for purposes of participating in a program referred to in such paragraph—

   (I) only as a result of any determination by the State or district attorney that probable cause of a bad check violation under State penal law exists, and that contact with the alleged offender for purposes of participation in the program is appropriate; and

   (II) the alleged offender has failed to pay the bad check after demand for payment, pursuant to State law, is made for payment of the check amount;

(v) includes as part of an initial written communication with an alleged offender a clear and conspicuous statement that—

   (I) the alleged offender may dispute the validity of any alleged bad check violation;

   (II) where the alleged offender knows, or has reasonable cause to believe, that the alleged bad check violation is the result of theft or forgery of the check, identity theft, or other fraud that is not the result of the conduct of the alleged offender, the alleged offender may file a crime report with the appropriate law enforcement agency; and

   (III) if the alleged offender notifies the private entity or the district attorney in writing, not later than 30 days after being contacted for the first time pursuant to clause (iv), that there is a dispute pursuant to this subsection, before further restitution efforts are pursued, the district attorney or an employee of the district attorney authorized to make such a determination makes a determination that there is probable cause to believe that a crime has been committed; and

(vi)   charges only fees in connection with services under the contract that have been authorized by the contract with the State or district attorney.

(b)   Certain Checks Excluded.—A check is described in this subsection if the check involves, or is subsequently found to involve—

(1)   a postdated check presented in connection with a payday loan, or other similar transaction, where the payee of the check knew that the issuer had insufficient funds at the time the check was made, drawn, or delivered;

(2)   a stop payment order where the issuer acted in good faith and with reasonable cause in stopping payment on the check;

(3)   a check dishonored because of an adjustment to the issuer's account by the financial institution holding such account without providing notice to the person at the time the check was made, drawn, or delivered;

(4)   a check for partial payment of a debt where the payee had previously accepted partial payment for such debt;

(5)   a check issued by a person who was not competent, or was not of legal age, to enter into a legal contractual obligation at the time the check was made, drawn, or delivered; or

(6)   a check issued to pay an obligation arising from a transaction that was illegal in the jurisdiction of the State or district attorney at the time the check was made, drawn, or delivered.

(c) Definitions—For purposes of this section, the following definitions shall apply:

    (1) STATE OR DISTRICT ATTORNEY—The term "State or district attorney" means the chief elected or appointed prosecuting attorney in a district, county (as defined in section 2 of title 1, United States Code), municipality, or comparable jurisdiction, including State attorneys general who act as chief elected or appointed prosecuting attorneys in a district, county (as so defined), municipality or comparable jurisdiction, who may be referred to by a variety of titles such as district attorneys, prosecuting attorneys, commonwealth's attorneys, solicitors, county attorneys, and state's attorneys, and who are responsible for the prosecution of State crimes and violations of jurisdiction-specific local ordinances.

    (2) CHECK—The term "check" has the same meaning as in section 3(6) of the Check Clearing for the 21st Century Act.

    (3) BAD CHECK VIOLATION—The term "bad check violation" means a violation of the applicable State criminal law relating to the writing of dishonored checks.

Appendix B

Glossary of Terms

As you engage in the process of settling your debts, you are likely to encounter many terms that you may not understand. I have included this glossary to help clear up some of those terms. The terms included here have either been used in this kit or they have been thrown around by debt collectors or attorneys during settlement discussions over the years.

I have also included a number of legal terms in this glossary. If you are sued by a creditor, you are likely to encounter many of these terms. The sources of most of the definitions have been included as well.

1099-C—The tax form filed with the IRS by a creditor, when $600 or more has been forgiven on a debt. IRS Web site www.irs.gov

admission—A statement made by a party to a lawsuit or by a criminal defendant, usually prior to trial, that certain facts are true. An admission is not to be confused with a confession of blame or guilt, but admits only some facts. *Law.com*

answer—1) A formal, written statement by the defendant in a lawsuit, which answers each allegation contained in the complaint. www.id.uscourts.gov/glossary.htm 2) A defendant's written response to a plaintiff's initial court filing (called a complaint or petition); normally, a defendant has thirty days in which to file an answer after being served with the plaintiff's complaint. In some courts, an answer is simply called a "response." *Nolo's Plain English Law Dictionary*

appearance—The act of coming into court as a party to a suit either in person or through an attorney. *Glossary of Legal Terms*, www.id.uscourts.gov/glossary.htm

arbitration—The hearing of a dispute by an impartial third person or persons (chosen by the parties), whose award the parties agree to accept. *Glossary of Legal Terms*, www.id.uscourts.gov/glossary.htm

award [of arbitration]— To give a judgment of money to a party to a lawsuit, arbitration, or administrative claim. Example: "Plaintiff is awarded $27,000." *Glossary of Legal Terms*, www.id.uscourts.gov/glossary.htm

arbitration notice—Formal notification to the party that has been sued in a civil case of the fact that the arbitration has been filed. Also, any form of notification of a legal proceeding. *Glossary of Legal Terms*, www.id.uscourts.gov/glossary.htm

arbitration response—See **answer**.

assets—The entire property of a person, association, corporation, or estate applicable or subject to the payment of debts. *Merriam-Webster Online Dictionary*

award—to give by the decision of a law court or arbitrator—"the plaintiff was *awarded* damages." *Webster's New World Dictionary*

bonds— In finance, usually a formal certificate of indebtedness issued in writing by governments or business corporations in return for loans. It bears interest and promises to pay a certain sum of money to the holder after a definite period, usually ten to twenty years. www.infoplease.com

budget—1) An estimate, often itemized, of expected income and expense for a given period in the future.
2) A plan of operations based on such an estimate.
3) An itemized allotment of funds, time, etc., for a given period. www.infoplease.com

cease and desist letter—*When a collector is harassing a consumer, the consumer may send a letter demanding that the creditor put an end to or refrain from those unfair actions. Sending such a letter can be an effective means of reducing the number of phone calls from collectors. The American Heritage® Dictionary of the English Language, Fourth Edition*

charge off—A debt that is deemed uncollectable and written off. Also known as a bad debt. www.investopedia.com

collection—The act or process of collecting. *The American Heritage*® *Dictionary of the English Language, Fourth Edition*

collection agency—See **collection**. The *Webster's New World Dictionary* defines agency as "the business of any person, firm, etc., empowered to act for another." Therefore a "collection agency" is a person or firm empowered to collect debts for another person or firm.

complaint—Papers filed with a court clerk by the plaintiff to initiate a lawsuit by setting out facts and legal claims. To complete the initial stage of a lawsuit, the plaintiff's complaint must be served on the defendant, who then has the opportunity to respond by filing an answer. *Nolo's Plain English Law Dictionary*

compound interest: interest on borrowing and accrued interest— Interest that is calculated on the combined total of the original sum borrowed (principal) and the interest it has already accrued. *Encarta World Dictionary*

conference hearing—See **hearing**. Sometimes brief sessions prior to the trial are called **conference hearings** to distinguish them from the actual trial hearings.

consent judgment—A judgment issued by a judge based on an agreement between the parties to a lawsuit to settle the matter, aimed at ending the litigation with a judgment that is enforceable. www.law.com

credit/pay-later system—An arrangement by which a buyer can take possession of something now and pay for it later or over time. *Encarta World Dictionary*

credit history/credit track record—A record of how somebody has repaid loans, credit card bills, and other debts in the past, used as a guide for any conditions on lending to them again. *Encarta World Dictionary*

creditor—A person or organization owed money by another. *Encarta World Dictionary*

collector—A person whose work is collecting taxes, overdue bills, etc. *Webster's New World Dictionary, Fourth College Edition*

debit—A charge against a bank deposit account. Can also refer to an entry showing a debt or expense in a record of accounts, or an amount of money taken out of an account. www.meriamwebster.com

debt to income ratio—The amount you owe measured against the amount make. The more you make, the more debt you can afford to take on. The following gives some parameters for comparison.

> **Debt-to-income ratios**
> **36 percent or less:** This is a healthy debt load to carry for most people.
> **37–42 percent:** Not bad, but start paring debt now before you get in real trouble.
> **43–49 percent:** Financial difficulties are probably imminent unless you take immediate action.
> **50 percent or more:** Get professional help to aggressively reduce debt.
> Source: Gerri Detweiler, author of *The Ultimate Credit Handbook*
> www.usnews.com/usnews/nycu/money/modebtratio.htm

debtor—Somebody who or something that owes a debt. *Encarta World Dictionary*

default—A failure to meet an obligation, especially a financial one. *Encarta World Dictionary*

default judgment—If a defendant in a lawsuit fails to respond to a complaint in the time set by law (commonly twenty or thirty days), then the plaintiff (suer) can request that the default (failure) be entered into the court record by the clerk, which gives the plaintiff the right to get a default judgment. A defendant who fails to file an answer or other legal response when it is due can request that the default be set aside, but must show a legitimate excuse and a good defense to the lawsuit. www.law.com

defendant: accused party—A person, party, or company required to answer criminal or civil charges in a court. *Encarta World Dictionary*

discovery—The stage of a legal proceeding during which each side must provide data and documents to the other side. *Encarta World Dictionary*

document hearing—In Document Hearings, the Arbitrator reviews documents or property to render an Order or Award. Parties do not appear at Document Hearings. www.adrforum.com

equity—The value of a piece of property over and above any mortgage or other liabilities relating to it. *Encarta World Dictionary*

expense—The amount of money spent in order to buy or do something. *Encarta World Dictionary*

FICO score—A FICO score is a credit score developed by Fair Isaac & Co. Credit scoring is a method of determining the likelihood that credit users will pay their bills. Fair Isaac began its pioneering work with credit scoring in the late 1950s and, since then, scoring has become widely accepted by lenders as a reliable means of credit evaluation. A credit score attempts to condense a borrower's credit history into a single number. Fair Isaac & Co. and the credit bureaus do not reveal exactly how these scores are computed. The Federal Trade Commission has ruled this to be acceptable.

Credit scores are calculated by using scoring models and mathematical tables that assign points for different pieces of information that best predict future credit performance. Developing these models involves studying how thousands, even millions, of people have used credit. Score-model developers find predictive factors in the data that have proven to indicate future credit performance. Models can be developed from different sources of data. Credit bureau models are developed from information in consumer credit-bureau reports. www.mtg-net.com/sfaq/faq/fico.htm

FTC/Federal Trade Commission—A federal body that oversees the act of consumer fraud, misleading advertising, credit cards, or other consumer protection matters, as well as antitrust or competition matters. FTC Web site, www.ftc.gov

hardship—Difficulty or suffering caused by a lack of something, especially money. *Encarta World Dictionary*

hearing—Any proceeding before a judge or other magistrate (such as a hearing officer or court commissioner) without a jury in which evidence and/or argument is presented to determine some issue of fact or both issues of fact and law. While technically a trial with a judge sitting without a jury fits the definition, a hearing usually refers to brief sessions involving a specific question at some time prior to the trial itself, or such specialized proceedings as administrative hearings. www.law.com

insolvency—the inability to pay debts. *Encarta World Dictionary*

interest—A charge made for a loan or credit facility, or a payment made by a bank or other financial institution for the use of money deposited in an account. *Encarta World Dictionary*

interrogatories—A set of written questions to a party to a lawsuit asked by the opposing party as part of the pre-trial discovery process. These questions must be answered in writing under oath or under penalty of perjury within a specified time (such as thirty days). www.law.com

investment—An outlay of money, for example, by depositing it in a bank or by buying stock in a company, with the object of making a profit. *Encarta World Dictionary*

invoice—A written record of goods or services provided and the amount charged for them, sent to a customer as a request for payment. *Encarta World Dictionary*

judgment—
> 1) **verdict**—The decision arrived at and pronounced by a court of law.
> 2) **obligation resulting from a verdict**—An obligation such as a debt that arises as a result of a court's verdict, or a document setting out an obligation of this kind.
> 3) **decision of a judge**—the decision reached by one or more judges in a contest. *Encarta World Dictionary*

lawsuit—A common term for a legal action by one person or entity against another person or entity, to be decided in a court of law, sometimes just called a "suit." www.law.com

levy—To seize property in order to satisfy a judgment. Often used with *on.* www.law.com

liability—One of the most significant words in the field of law, liability means legal responsibility for one's acts or omissions. Failure of a person or entity to meet that responsibility leaves him/her/it open to a lawsuit for any resulting damages or to a court order to perform (as in a breach of contract or violation of statute). In order to win a lawsuit, the suing party (plaintiff) must prove the legal liability of the defendant if the plaintiff's allegations are shown to be true. This requires evidence of the duty to act, the failure to fulfill that duty and the connection (proximate cause) of that failure to some injury or harm to the plaintiff. Liability also applies to alleged criminal acts in which the defendant may be responsible for his/her acts that constitute a crime, thus making him/her subject to conviction and punishment. Example: Jack Jumpstart runs a stop sign in his car and hits Sarah Stepforth as she is crossing in the cross-walk. Jack has a duty of care to Sarah (and the public) that he breaches by his negligence, and therefore he has liability for Sarah's injuries, giving her the right to bring a lawsuit against him. However, Jack's father owns the automobile and he, too, may have liability to Sarah based on a statute that makes a car owner liable for any damages caused by the vehicle he owns. The father's responsibility is based on "statutory liability," even though he personally breached no duty. A signer of a promissory note has liability for money due if it is not paid and so would a cosigner who guarantees it. A contractor who has agreed to complete a building has liability to the owner if he fails to complete it on time. www.law.com

lien—Any official claim or charge against property or funds for payment of a debt or an amount owed for services rendered. A lien is usually a formal document signed by the party to whom money is owed and sometimes by the debtor who agrees to the amount due. A lien carries with it the right to sell property, if necessary, to obtain the money. A mortgage or a deed of trust is a form of lien, and any lien against real property must be recorded with the county recorder to be enforceable, including an abstract of judgment, which turns a judgment into a lien against the judgment debtor's property. There are numerous types of liens, including a mechanic's lien against the real property upon which a workman, contractor, or supplier has provided work or materials; an attorney's lien for fees to be paid from funds recovered by his/her efforts; a medical lien for medical bills to be paid from funds recovered for an injury; a landlord's lien against a tenant's property for unpaid rent or damages; a tax lien to enforce the government's claim of unpaid taxes; or the security agreement (UCC-1) authorized by the Uniform Commercial Code. Most liens are enforceable in the order in which they were recorded or filed (in the case of security agreements), except tax liens, which have priority over the private citizen's claim. www.law.com

mutual funds—A mutual fund brings together money from many people and invests it in stocks, bonds, or other assets. Individual investors own shares of the fund, and the fund owns the stocks, bonds, or other assets it invests in.

negotiation—(often pl.) A conferring, discussing, or bargaining to reach agreement. *Webster's New World Dictionary, Fourth College Edition*

order—1) Every direction or mandate of a judge or a court which is not a judgment or legal opinion (although both may include an order) directing that something be done or that there is prohibition against some act. This can range from an order that a case will be tried on a certain date, to an order that a convicted defendant be executed at the state prison. 2) When a judge directs that a party before the court perform a particular act or refrain from certain acts or directs a public official or court employee (like a sheriff) to take certain actions, such as seizing property or arresting an AWOL defendant. www.law.com

per annum—By the year; annually. www.law.com

petition—1) A formal written request to a court for an order of the court. It is distinguished from a complaint in a lawsuit that asks for damages and/or performance by the opposing party. Petitions include demands for writs, orders to show cause, modifications of prior orders, continuances, dismissal of a case, reduction of bail in criminal cases, a decree of distribution of an estate, appointment of a guardian, and a host of other matters arising in legal actions. 2) A general term for a writing signed by a number of people asking for a particular result from a private governing body (such as a homeowners association, a political party, or a club). 3) In public law, a writing signed by a number of people that is required to place a proposition or ordinance on the ballot, nominate a person for public office, or demand a recall election. Such petitions for official action must be signed by a specified number of registered voters (such as five percent). 4) To make a formal request of a court; to present a written request to an organization's governing body, signed by one or more members. 5) A suit for divorce in some states, in which the parties are called petitioner and respondent. www.law.com

plaintiff— The party who initiates a lawsuit by filing a complaint with the clerk of the court against the defendant(s) demanding damages, performance, and/or court determination of rights. www.law.com

pre-trial conference—A meeting of two or more persons to discuss specific issues before a trial begins.

pre-trial hearing—In criminal law, a "preliminary hearing" is held before a judge to determine whether the prosecutor has presented sufficient evidence that the accused has committed a crime to hold him/her for trial. www.law.com

pro per—Synonymous with *pro se*. (See next.)

pro se—The term used to describe a party that participates in a legal proceeding without an attorney. publicservice.vermont.gov/Lamoille/glossary-legal.htm

property lien—See **lien**.

refinance—To provide new financing or new financing for, as by discharging a mortgage with the proceeds from a new mortgage obtained at a lower interest rate. *The American Heritage® Dictionary of the English Language, Fourth Edition*

response—See **answer**.

settle—To resolve (a dispute) by agreement between the parties.

settlement—An agreement, arrangement, or adjustment. *Webster's New World Dictionary, Fourth College Edition*

statements—A summary of a financial account showing the balance on deposit or balance due. www.meriamwebster.com

stay—A court-ordered, short-term delay in judicial proceedings to give a losing defendant time to arrange for payment of the judgment or to move out of the premises in an unlawful detainer case. www.law.com

stipulation—An agreement, usually on a procedural matter, between the attorneys for the two sides in a legal action. Some stipulations are oral, but the courts often require that the stipulation be put in writing, signed, and filed with the court. www.law.com

stocks—

1. The capital or fund that a corporation raises through the sale of shares, entitling the stockholder to dividends and to other rights of ownership, such as voting rights.
2. The number of shares that each stockholder possesses.
3. A stock certificate.
4. The part of a tally or record of account formerly given to a creditor.
5. A debt symbolized by a tally. www.yourdictionary.com

summary judgment—A court order ruling that no factual issues remain to be tried and therefore a cause of action or all causes of action in a complaint can be decided upon certain facts without trial. A summary judgment is based upon a motion by one of the parties that contends that all necessary factual issues are settled or so one-sided they need not be tried. The motion is supported by declarations under oath, excerpts from depositions which are under oath, admissions of fact and other discovery, as well as a legal argument (points and authorities), that argue that there are no triable issues of fact and that the settled facts require a summary judgment for the moving party. The opposing party will respond by counter-declarations and legal arguments attempting to show that there are "triable issues of fact." If it is unclear whether there is a triable issue of fact in any cause of action, then summary judgment must be denied as to that cause of action. The theory behind the summary judgment process is to eliminate the need to try settled factual issues and to decide without trial one or more causes of action in the complaint. The pleading procedures are extremely technical and complicated and are particularly dangerous to the party against whom the motion is made. www.law.com

summons—A document issued by the court at the time a lawsuit is filed, stating the name of both plaintiff and defendant, the title and file number of the case, the court and its address, the name and address of the plaintiff's attorney, and instructions as to the need to file a response to the complaint within a certain time (such as thirty days after service), usually with a form on the back on which information of service of summons and complaint is to be filled out and signed by the process server. A copy of the summons must be served on each defendant at the same time as the complaint to start the time running for the defendant to answer. Certain writs and orders to show cause are served instead of a summons since they contain the same information along with special orders of the court. After service to the defendants, the original summons, along with the "return of service" proving the summons and complaint were served, is filed with the court to show that each defendant was served. A summons differs from a subpoena, which is an order to a witness to appear. www.law.com

trial—The examination of facts and law presided over by a judge (or other magistrate, such as a commissioner or judge *pro tem*) with authority to hear the matter (jurisdiction). www.law.com

withholdings—To deduct (withholding tax) from income. www.meriamwebster.com

writ—A written order of a judge requiring specific action by the person or entity to whom the writ is directed. www.law.com

writ of execution—A court order to a sheriff to enforce a judgment by levying on real or personal property of a judgment debtor to obtain funds to satisfy the judgment amount (in order to pay the winning plaintiff). www.law.com

writ of garnishment—See **writ**.